REMARKS

R.E.M.

THE STORY OF R.E.M.

Omnibus Press LONDON – NEW YORK – SYDNEY – COLOGNE

D1333757

tony fletcher

© Copyright 1989 Omnibus Press
(A Division of Book Sales Limited)

Edited by **Chris Charlesworth**
Designed by **Liz Nicholson**
Artwork by **Tim Field**
Picture research **by Debbie Dorman and
Tony Fletcher**
Cover photography by **Tom Sheehan**
Typeset by **Capital Setters, London**
Printed in Scotland by **The Eagle Press PLC,
Blantyre, Glasgow**

ISBN 0.7119.1813.9
Order No. OP 45442

Exclusive distributors:

Book Sales Limited,
8/9 Frith Street,
London W1V 5TZ, UK.

Music Sales Pty Limited,
120 Rothschild Avenue,
Rosebery, NSW 2018, Australia.

To the Music Trade only:
Music Sales Limited,
8/9 Frith Street,
London W1V 5TZ, UK.

Omnibus Press is grateful to **Dominic Martin**
for the loan of record sleeves and memorabilia
to illustrate this book.

'REMARKS' initially sprang from a desire to home in on a story that seemed worth the telling. I was aware from the beginning that attempting to unravel the mystery of R.E.M. might well involve clutching at intangibles, and while at the project's conclusion, it seems to me as obvious as ever that the secret of R.E.M.'s success is exactly that – an indefinable chemistry that just *is* – that does not make the story any the less exciting. Following the trail of their decade-long adventure was a delightful journey that I hope is successfully recounted over the ensuing pages.

As I was not privy to R.E.M.'s early exploits, I decided to let the characters involved help tell the story in their own words. To this end I interviewed dozens of key players, all of whom are either quoted or mentioned somewhere within. My thanks to every one of them for their time and their memories.

On the occasions that these recollections were vague, or two opinions differed, I attempted to ascertain the facts by drawing on further opinions or finding printed evidence. Rock 'n' roll being the minefield of uncontrollable egos and joyous myth-making that it is, this sometimes proved to be a difficult exercise, but I will stand by my conclusions.

To R.E.M., I must offer thanks for not slamming the door shut after the initial refusal of co-operation. I understand why a group perhaps only halfway through an existence built on enigma should not want to bare its soul in print and destroy the mystery and I am glad that everyone came to understand how and why I wanted to write this book, finally granting interviews without pre-conditions (even if that did involve a hazardous journey through Buckland!). My thanks to Bill, Mike, Michael and Peter for the music; Jefferson and Bert for being easy to deal with; and Liz Hammond, Debbie Kilpatrick and Brooke Johnson for efficiency. Thanks to everyone I briefly encountered on tour who helped.

For R.E.M. archive material, I would like to thank hardened collectors Fred Mills, 'Mad' Louie, Patti Kleinke, Andy Johnson, Bryan Cook, Annie Fort at I.R.S., and everyone else who supplied me with tapes or cuttings.

My stay in Athens would not have been such a pleasure without the wonderful hospitality of Carolyn Overton, Robin Taylor and Mary Gambrell. Equally fun to be around in Athens were Mark Baldovski, Terry and Trent Allen, Drew Worsham, Mark Cline and Mike Richmond, along with many, many others I hope not to fall out of touch with.

To Ira Robbins, who sent me The New Trouser Press Record Guide in the hope that I would review it, I can only say that I am not sure how accurately I could have told this story without it. A superb reference book.

Thanks to Scott Schinder, Susan Myers and Melissa Manuel of The Dixie Voice, Karen Moss, and Steve Fallon for various assistance.

Despite the many and extensive interviews I undertook in the research of this book, I occasionally found it necessary to use a quote from another source to best make a point. These quotes were taken from the interviews conducted by the following people: Bill Black (Sounds 4/84), Laurent Chalumeau (Rapido 11/88), Matt Damsker (San Diego Union 6/83), Anthony De Curtis (Record 7/85, Rolling Stone 8/87, 4/89), Adrian Deevoy (Q, 12/88), Harold De Muir (East Coast Rocker 10/87, NME 11/88), Bill Flanagan (Musician 1/88), Bill Forman (Bam 10/86), David Fricke (Musician 7/84), Don Gilliand (Ft. Lauderdale Rag 5/83), Marty Graham (Milwaukee Express 6/83), Robert Hilburn (Los Angeles Times 6/85), Bill Holdship (Creem 9/85), Allan Jones (Melody Maker 6/85), Sean O'Hagan (NME 12/88), Hugh Morley (Jamming 1/85), John Morthland (Xtra 6/85), Jeff Nesin (Creem 9/84), John Platt (Bucketful of Brains #11, 84), Steve Pond (Rolling Stone 12/87), Edwin Pouncey (Sounds 10/88), Karen Schlossberg (Creem 12/87), Mat Smith (Melody Maker 9/87), Jim Sullivan (Record 7/83), Jeff Tamarkin (Creem 9/84), Rob Tannenbaum (Centrum Guide 85), Ed Ward (Austin American-Statesman 6/83) and Jon Young (Trouser Press 8/83).

To the person who one day attempts the definitive critical biography of Michael Stipe – although I suggest they wait a few years – I offer good luck. You will need it!

Finally, in the prevailing circumstances, this book would not have been possible without Ruth and Adria, whose enthusiasm, understanding and physical assistance will never be forgotten. Thank you.

■ ■ ■

■ The very first public performance of R.E.M.,

at the church on Oconee Street,

(Sandra-Lee Phipps)

Saturday April 5, 1980.

The Church (Caryn L. Rose)

(Sandra-Lee Phipps)

Athens, Georgia, April 5 1980

All week long, the word had been passed around town. Party this Saturday. Three live bands. Free beer. Now, with hundreds of people converging upon the old Episcopal church on Oconee Street, just around the corner from the University of Georgia, the Athens grapevine was once again proven unfailingly effective.

That the party location had been intended as a house of worship was verified by the steeple rising forty feet high and towering above rooftops further up the hill. But no religious service had been held here in many a year, not since the dilapidated building had been converted into the most bizarre living quarters a student could imagine.

Once past the front doors in fact, it was impossible to determine that one was indeed inside a church. Instead, a large open plan living room and kitchen gave way to an insalubrious bathroom on one side and a bedroom on the other, in between which a staircase led up to four more rooms, each just big enough to throw down a mattress, some clothes, and a few books.

However, by crawling through the closet at the back of the downstairs bedroom, one came across the entire, undeveloped rear half of what undoubtedly *was* a church. A floor space some thirty feet wide and twenty feet deep lay in front of a low-rise altar, from which, by facing back inwards, the thin plasterboard walls erected to create the two-tiered living quarters were clearly visible, a cardboard box inside a house of God. Now, the altar was festooned with guitars, amplifiers and drums; tonight, it would baptise the three latest members of Athens' already extensive musical family.

To prevent theft of what few possessions the tenants had, the front doors to the church were locked this Saturday evening. Partygoers duly walked around back and through the rear entrance intended for choirboys and preachers, or simply climbed through the holes in the wall that had once been majestic church windows. Some chose to crawl through the closet and join selected revellers inside the apartment; others stayed outside throughout, enjoying the warm night air.

Turtle Bay were the first group to perform; they were followed by The Side Effects, a trio of popular art students whose infectious, angular dance rhythms were an instant hit. By the time the final band appeared, the party was reaching a drunken climax, the police had already made a threatening appearance, and the quality of music was of only marginal importance.

This last group had not even decided on a name, so new were they, and no one had a firm idea what to expect. But the partygoers all recognised at least one face in the band. The guitarist, Peter Buck, was a music-obsessed rocker who worked behind the counter at the town's major record store, Wuxtry. The singer, Michael Stipe, was a soft-spoken art student whose retiring nature made it all the more surprising that he should now be throwing himself about the stage with such abandon. Both lived at the church. The rhythm section, boyish bassist Mike Mills and thickset drummer Bill Berry, were close friends from Macon whose party spirits had quickly endeared them to the locals.

As a unit, they were fast, furious and sloppy, making up in energy what they lacked in expertise. People danced, drank and sang along when they recognised a sixties trash-pop gem like 'Stepping Stone'. Others frowned upon the proliferation of cover songs: in a community with such a strong reputation for art, innovation was a virtual necessity for performing. Such doubts were but quietly mooted, however: after all, the band were their friends and the show was a shitload of fun. They even called them back for an encore, a dilemma for a band that had run out of songs, and one they solved by calling their friends onstage to sing easy-to-play oldies. As rotting floorboards began to crack under the pressure, Michael Stipe ended the performance by crawling among the audience on his hands and knees.

Outside, the sun was already coming up. A new day was dawning in Athens, Georgia.

■ ■ ■

T

The City of Athens lies an hour and a half's drive east of the Georgia state capital Atlanta, its tree-lined avenues of sturdy ante-bellum homes and glorious neo-classical mansions bearing all the trademarks of a quintessentially quaint southern American town. A place where time would seem to stand still, with sultry summer afternoons spent lazing on the front porch, and the Baptist church forever the dominant political force.

■ **Jim Herbert, painter, photographer and film maker. Responsible for many of R.E.M.'s videos.** (Andy Sharp)

This elegant impression is accurate, but it is merely the freeze frame of the picture postcard; start the camera rolling and a storyline of confrontation and flux unfolds. It is a saga involving some 50,000 permanent citizens, ranging from the inheritors of old money to the perpetually poor, and a floating population of 20,000 students. For Athens is also a college town, home to the University Of Georgia and the attendant behaviour that can be found wherever teenagers – especially those suddenly freed from the shackles of family life – congregate. Athens has always enjoyed a heady reputation for partying, but for years this was shielded behind a façade of austerity, as indicated by the outwardly pristine mile of fraternity and sorority houses on Milledge Avenue. Even during the supposedly 'swinging' mid-sixties, the University forbade such trivial activities as smoking on campus or lounging on the grass.

When at last the wind of change blew through Athens, it did so with force. Some attribute it to the provocative and liberating climate of the era, others to the establishment of the University's Department of Art as the best in the south-east. Either way, towards the end of the sixties a new breed of creative student began emerging on campus: the hippy.

Among the faculty members thankful for its arrival and positive input was Jim Herbert, a painter, art instructor and film maker living in Athens since 1962 who recalls a "clash of the rednecks and the hippies" with relish. "When the hippy thing did hit here, it was extremely strong and very poignant," he says. "Kids roaming around the streets with musical instruments, parties with nude people . . ."

The hippies and their lifestyle left an indelible imprint on Athens culture, and from the late '60's onwards, the Department of Art's reputation ensured that each new year brought with it freshmen eager to immerse themselves in a thriving artistic community. That they were unable to conquer the inherent conservatism of the University structure became increasingly irrelevant as they created a community of their own.

Among the new art students arriving in 1975 was Curtis Crowe, who recalls finding "a real good art school party crowd. There was a certain camaraderie just because you were in the art school; you had an instant affiliation with these people."

These new friendships extended beyond the classroom into a party scene that brought the adventurous students and progressive instructors closer together. These were theatrical parties, afternoon lawn gatherings with unique costumes and bizarre behaviour, and some of the best were thrown by the art professors themselves. Yet despite such artistic activity, Athens offered no music scene for those who weren't into the southern boogie or laid back jazz that dominated the local clubs in the mid-seventies.

Up in New York, the story was different: a new musical movement was emerging from darkened Lower East Side clubs, one which dispelled the accepted notions of musical expertise as a pre-requisite for performance. It was a disparate scene, ranging from the nihilistic thrash of The Ramones at one end to the staccato art pop of Talking Heads at the other, but it carried a unanimous ethos: anyone can do it.

This dictum would soon inspire a generation of bored teenagers in Britain to seize the initiative and launch an aggressive punk rock movement – one that would briefly prove as threatening to society as the hippies of a decade earlier, before settling into a vague musical niche termed 'new wave' – but when word of New York's musical stirring reached the Athens art crowd, they were attracted more by the beauty of its possibilities than the anger of its defiance.

Unsurprisingly, the first to realise these opportunities were among the town's most celebrated characters. Cindy Wilson, her brother Ricky and Keith Strickland had grown up in Athens; Kate Pierson and Fred Schneider had arrived later and never left. Together, they were renowned "party terrorists", gatecrashers in garish outfits fond of starting food fights or, in Kate's case, known to soak unsuspecting guests with a commandeered garden hose. "We were just free spirits," she recalls.

Now they were all looking for a way out of dead-end jobs. Over a drunken Chinese meal one night, they decided to form a band, naming it the B-52's after local slang for the girls' bouffant wigs. Combining their effervescent personal traits with the comic book vocals of Fred, Cindy and Kate, and an irrepressible dance beat, they hit on a sensational formula.

With "no place for us to play live except for friends' living rooms," as Fred Schneider recalls, they made their public début at a St. Valentine's Day party in 1977. After four or five such events, Atlanta's premier punk band The Fans invited them along for the ride to New York, where they were playing in November '77. The 'B's' left with a tape and returned with a date, at the prestigious club Max's Kansas City on December 12. The night before leaving, they played a party hosted by Curtis Crowe's room-mate.

"To me, it was culture shock," recalls Curtis. "It was a kind of frightening experience for a neophyte to go and see the B-52's, and it wasn't so much the band. The entire crowd was so dramatically different from your average run-of-the-mill crowd of people; the entire crowd was the show.

"The B-52's really touched the spark to the keg of dynamite. They created what is known as the Athens music scene."

Before 1977 was out, the B-52's played a party at Emory University's Student Center in Atlanta, and a crowd of Athens socialites made the journey with them. Their host that night was a gregarious young music fan by the name of Peter Buck.

■ ■ ■

Peter Buck's life had always revolved around music. Yet he had never seriously considered making it his profession. He didn't have the talent, and he couldn't find anyone with his tastes and opinions. It was that simple.

Born in Los Angeles on December 6 1956, Buck spent his formative years in the suburbs of San Francisco. His love affair with pop music began, as for so many, with a transistor radio and the thrill of listening under the pillow to magical sounds from faraway places: Britain's fab four The Beatles, Motown goddesses The Supremes, and television stars The Monkees.

San Francisco during the sixties was an exciting place to live, glazy-eyed beatniks roaming streets that would later become the mecca of the hippy movement. And school was progressive, his class of eight-year-olds being treated one day to a performance by an identikit sixties pop group called The Postmen who played the latest Beatles and Byrds hits. Peter didn't have to be told the titles of the songs: every last dime he could talk out of his parents was already going towards buying records.

When the Buck family moved to Indiana, the free concerts and street culture became a thing of the past, and by the time they finally settled in Roswell, Georgia, in 1970, his parents might have expected Peter to have shaken off his infatuation with pop music. But their now teenage son's tastes had only matured and hardened; he was reading the

serious rock press and buying albums by The Kinks, The Move and The Stones. By rights, he should have then followed his peers into the hard rock that dominated the early seventies, but his love of pop led him instead to gorge on the British glam rock of T. Rex, Slade, and Sweet.

Roswell was hardly the obvious place to indulge such eclectic tastes. Though a mere eighteen miles from the centre of Atlanta, Peter recalls it as "a separate town, like living way out in the country." Gentrification during the eighties has turned it into just another pleasant suburb, but back then "It was all old Dairy Queens and guys in overalls with hay in the back of their battered pickup trucks, poking through town and spitting tobacco juice on the sidewalk." The opening of a McDonalds in Roswell was considered a major cultural advancement; the young Buck couldn't wait to get out.

■ **The Velvet Underground** (Pictorial Press)

Two events during the artistically bleak mid-seventies helped him define his future. The first was discovering an old Velvet Underground record in a garage sale. Their sound was so simple and direct, so haunting and so timeless that it taught Peter Buck to value understated repetition more than overblown polyphony.

The second was witnessing the New York Dolls in concert in the mid seventies. The Dolls were the bastard offspring of glam rock, an overwhelmingly vile and aggressive group commercially shunned during their short tenure as major label artists. But their rawness convinced Buck that power need not be born out of accomplishment.

The seeds of making music were planted in his mind. But although Peter Buck understood the rudiments of the guitar, he was deterred from studying it properly by his only brother Kenny who, at two years younger than him, was a classically trained prodigy whose skills made Peter's attempts look embarrassing. A cheap guitar of his own that he took apart to paint was left in disrepair, and on the occasions Peter and friends did get together to jam, they never ventured beyond the twelve-bar blues.

Upon finishing high school in 1975, Peter enrolled at Emory University in Atlanta and decided to leave home as well. His father gave him two parting shots of advice: 'Don't get married before you're thirty, no matter what happens; and don't get into showbiz, it'll only break your heart.' The first of these his son kept to; the second would fall by the wayside, but only over a period of time. For while playing music was becoming an increasingly attractive proposition, and Peter purchased a decent guitar, finding suitable partners was a nigh impossible task.

"By and large, almost everyone you'd meet in a band in the seventies wanted to be rich and famous like Rod Stewart, and already had that attitude," he recalls. "You'd just think, 'What a bunch of assholes.'" This attitude didn't endear him to fellow students. "I was kind of stand-offish at college. I looked down my nose at everyone. All these people were into the Grateful Dead and Hot Tuna and Little Feat."

Peter's own musical taste buds were by now absorbing the new underground rock from New York. The same corner of the same big city that gave birth to the Velvet Underground and New York Dolls was beginning to spew out a whole generation of left-field talent. The first visible example was female punk-poet Patti Smith, whose 1975 debut 'Horses' sounded like nothing else before it. When she came to Atlanta on her first tour, Buck saw every one of her shows. The experience only served to further convince him that he was wasting his time at University. After less than one full year of classes, he dropped out.

Buck had harboured ambitions of being a music critic, but this too seemed distant and unobtainable. The easiest way to earn a living off music was to work in a record store, and so he found himself behind the counter at Doo Dahs in Atlanta. There he was able to keep in step with the changing musical climate. The Ramones and Blondie released their début albums in 1976, and Talking Heads

and Television quickly followed suit with stunning singles. Buck absorbed them all. He also noted that British youth was responding with its own musical explosion. The names were as uncompromising as the music – The Sex Pistols, The Clash, The Damned – and here was he, thousands of miles away from the action.

Frustrated with Atlanta, he embarked on what he calls "that whole Jack Kerouac stuff", hitchhiking around America, sleeping rough when the need arose. He was washing dishes for a living in early 1977 in San Luis Obispo, California, staying with some "real big Grateful Dead fans", when he ordered The Sex Pistols' 'Anarchy In The UK' from a local import record store. "I took it home and played it, and totally horrified everybody. They thought Kiss was punk rock."

Returning to Georgia, he found the wheels of progress moving only very gradually. "Atlanta was always slow," he recalls. "I think because it's so widespread people didn't hang out together and do things." Browsing through the new releases at Wuxtry Records one day – "you had to search this stuff out; in 1977, you'd buy any record that was even vaguely punk," – his poise and knowledge attracted

■ **Patti Smith** (Arista)

the eye of the store's co-owner, Mark Methe, who offered Buck a job there and then. From his view back behind the record counter, Buck considered himself one of maybe just thirty people in the entire city who understood punk. They were the same thirty people who made up the audience at shows by The Fans.

Danny Beard was among them. Proprietor of another Atlanta record store called Wax 'n' Facts, he was a close friend of The Fans and a former resident of Athens. He had seen the B-52's play at Curtis Crowe's apartment there and, captivated, travelled with them on their first trip to New York. By the time they arrived back in Georgia, Danny had decided to launch his own 'DB Records' with a B-52's single. He had also offered to put on a party where they could debut in Atlanta, and Peter Buck, being a musical aficionado and to Danny's knowledge, still a student at Emory, seemed an ideal person to arrange it.

Buck and a student friend were happy to oblige, hiring the Student Center's impressive Coke Room for $25. Danny Beard sang the B-52's praises to every customer who passed through his shop, and come the night, in late December 1977, around 100 curious onlookers turned up to the hastily arranged free event.

It was a spectacular success: not only were the B-52's so much more original than the majority of Atlanta bands, but the crowd they brought with them were far more tuned in as well. So, when during that same Christmas week in 1977

■ **The B -52's** (Pictorial Press)

Mark Methe asked Peter whether he wanted to work in their Athens store, he accepted immediately. He handed over his apartment lease to Mark, swapped his Fender Stratocaster guitar for his boss's custom-built Telecaster, and moved in with his brother Kenny – who was already attending University in Athens – on the Lexington Highway, way out on the edge of town. Peter Buck celebrated a new year in a new home.

He was back in Atlanta within days for the historic American début of The Sex Pistols, opening their American tour on January 5 in what they saw as a provocative attack on the heart of the reactionary deep south. For the most part, their supposition was correct – the majority of the 600-strong audience at the Great Southeast Music Hall were media hounds, curious onlookers and threatening rednecks – but Buck was among the genuinely excited fans who had reserved tickets in advance. When he got there, however, he found that in the chaos of the event, they had been given to journalists flown down from New York.

Buck was livid. "I said, 'You mean these half-assed journalists got *my* tickets?' And I was with this guy who was just so furious – he was a big guy – he knocked the doorman down, kicked the door in, and stormed through. About four of us ran in while they were playing."

For the next ten minutes, Buck kept one eye on the stage and one eye on the bouncers pursuing him. "I was moving all the time. I was just trying to lose myself, but there was no chance, they knew who I was. I got to see about a song and a half before they dragged me out and punched me out on the curb. The guy I came with got to see the whole show. I got beaten up in the parking lot – not too badly, but they definitely kicked me around." He is not too disappointed now he looks back on it, pointing out that he enjoyed "pretty much the quintessential Sex Pistols experience."

While in Atlanta, Peter Buck's music tastes were considered eccentric, in Athens they were merely *au courant*. "Of course I worked in the hip record store," he notes, "So within two weeks I had all kinds of friends." Wuxtry had one shop close by the University in the heart of town, and one a ten minute walk west on Baxter Street. Both were consistently full of students, artists, and other young people with plenty of leisure time to soak up the newest music. Many of these customers were toying with the idea of forming bands themselves, and Peter joined them.

■ **Sex Pistols in USA 1978.** (Pictorial Press)

"The only thing I ever remember Pete doing," recalls his boss at Wuxtry in Athens, Dan Wall, "was sitting around playing guitar along with records." By Peter's own account, he could only play a beginner's 'open' chords, but Wall recalls him as being "fairly qualified by this point." The punk explosion allowed musical novices to get up on stage if they felt they had something to say, and talent was no longer the necessity it had been during Peter's teens; he thus found himself caught between acquiring the ability to improve and the thrill of no longer needing to.

This approach applied to his education too, temporarily resumed by taking classes in English, at which he excelled, and maths, at which he didn't, at night school. Essentially, Peter was just making the most of his new environment. He quicked garnered a reputation around town as a good friend and a bad enemy, with a girlfriend, Allison, who was his match in every department. Walking around with both a knife and a short temper persuaded most locals not to pursue an argument with him. Those who did had to be prepared to end it physically.

Towards the end of his first year in Athens, Peter began to recognise among the new visitors to Wuxtry a quietly-spoken teenager with good taste and two attractive females on his arm. "I thought, 'God! This guy's got two great looking girlfriends. He must be pretty hip.' " The girls were sisters, Lynda and Cyndy; the boy was their brother, Michael Stipe.

Although he was born in the Atlanta suburb of Decatur, on January 4 1960, John Michael Stipe felt like anything but a native Georgian when his family returned to the area in 1978. By then, he had little attachment to any place in particular, a sense of dislocation common to all children of army parentage. In Michael's case, his father's military career – which included a harrowing spell flying helicopters in Vietnam – took him through homes in Georgia, Texas, Germany, Illinois and Georgia again. When he later recalled that he "didn't touch base a lot during childhood," he exercised a rare poor choice of words, for his formative years revolved around the bases of the United States Armed Forces.

Army brats, as they are known, come to expect upheaval so frequently that they often consider the process of forming friendships pointless; instead, they become self-contained and introspective. Michael Stipe was a perfect example, a painfully shy child who preferred to observe rather than participate. Shunning outside companionship, he turned inward to the only constants in his life, his family: he and his sisters became the closest of friends.

The young Michael withdrew even further into himself when he entered high school while living in Collinsville, Illinois, just east of St. Louis. The brash behaviour of his fellow adolescents there overwhelmed him. "It was a very

■ ■ ■

outgoing, flamboyant, loud school and I hated everything about it," he later recalled. "I was very, kind of, *afraid* of a lot of things."

To provide his own entertainment and expand his knowledge, he subscribed to the New York cultural Bible, the *Village Voice*, in 1975. It was an opportune choice, for New York's downtown music scene was thriving, and the writers' excitement jumped off the page as they enthused about the new denizens of the underground.

Until now, music had hardly touched the fifteen-year-old's life: his parents' tastes revolved around the likes of Gershwin and Mancini, and his own record collection was all but non-existent. But the articles in the *Voice* were so powerful that when Patti Smith's début album 'Horses' was released in 1975, he bought it immediately. As he later recounted to the *New Musical Express*, he was not disappointed.

"It *killed*. It was so completely liberating. I had these headphones, my parents' crappy headphones and I sat up all night with a huge bowl of cherries listening to Patti Smith, eating those cherries and going 'Oh My God! . . . Holy Shit! . . . Fuck!' Then I was sick."

He was also converted. New York punk, he says, "immediately put into place everything everyone else in my school was listening to." He built a record collection of select substance, snapping up essential debut albums by Television and English art-punks Wire as they were released at one end, while following up on supposed influences such as The Stooges and New York Dolls at the other. When he acquired The Velvet Underground's live album '1969' for $2 in 1977, he was as astounded by their beautiful minimalism as his future partner Peter Buck had been before him.

As punk developed from an art form into a commodity, the other teenagers at his high school became attracted to it. Michael's musical knowledge accorded him popularity and, aided by the inherent confidence of adolescence, he became far more forceful a character, "this real loud, extreme, extroverted personality", as he later described it. He even fronted a short-lived punk band who performed on three occasions before his parents announced the family's move to Watkinsville, a small town ten miles south of Athens.

For Michael, this was a catastrophe. Not only was he finally enjoying life as a teenager in the metropolis of St Louis after years of self-doubt, but the family trips to his grandparents in Georgia – where his grandfather was a preacher – had convinced him that the state was 'full of hippies and southern boogie music'. To some extent he was right. But then Athens was not typical of Georgia.

Preconceptions being the powerful governing force they are, however, Michael Stipe withdrew back into his shell, becoming a 'troglodyte' – his own term –.on moving to Athens in 1978. That, he says, was a "particularly long and intense period" of shyness that he only came out of around 1984 – ironically, the very period that he began erecting barricades around his persona, giving a public impression of further withdrawal.

Most of his first year in Athens he spent by himself. "I just sat around reading or listening to music. That year alone, I think I really matured about five years . . . It's a long time to go without talking to people, and it really put a lot of things into perspective for me. I became much more of a quiet person after that. Much less bombastic, which is good."

The artistic instinct stronger than ever, Michael enrolled at the Department of Art in late 1978. Opinions on his ability and potential vary. Jim Herbert, who taught him on a freshman course has no recollections of Stipe the pupi whatsoever. Michael himself, meanwhile, modestly declares that "I was good at going to school but I wasn't good at what I was doing. I was able to convince my teachers that what I was doing was worthwhile when I was not really doing anything."

At least one of those teachers, Scott Belville, a respected artist who took Michael for a beginner's painting course, strongly disagrees. "He was actually one of the better students I ever had," he recalls. "You just looked at him and said 'This person is real talented.' " Belville noted and respected both his student's reserved temperament – "When he did have something to say, it carried a little more weight, because he was generally so quiet" – and his artistic talent.

"In a couple of paintings, something else came out that made you think, 'Wait a minute, this is much more mature work, much more interesting than you generally see in a beginning class.' " Belville even rescued two of Michael's discarded paintings from destruction, believing them to be of an exceptional quality. He describes them with adjectives that would frequently be used in reviews of his pupil's future lyrics: ''real brooding . . . a presence to them of another place . . . like a dream . . . abstract . . .''

During the course, Scott Belville convinced Michael Stipe to attend a show at the local Botanical Gardens by the eccentric Georgian folk artist, the Reverend Howard Finster. The student was fascinated by the old man's primitive sacred art and struck up a lasting relationship. Stipe also enrolled in a photo design course, the art form he was both most suited for and worked hardest on.

experienced a new emotional peak on discovering The Velvet Underground. On a personal level, however, they differed greatly: Peter was an outgoing, worldly-wise character more than three years older than the sensitive Michael. Perhaps recognising in Stipe's naïvete a refreshing antidote to his own blasé attitude, Buck nonetheless made a firm attempt to befriend his customer.

''Michael's got this great ability,'' says Peter. ''If he doesn't know something, he'll latch on to people and learn from them. He was new to town and he was learning things and meeting people.'' Peter would invite Michael out for drinks

■ **Michael Stipe at the University of Georgia Art Department in Athens, 1979, before the formation of R.E.M.** (Terry Allen)

In the meantime, he would regularly stop in at Wuxtry, enquiring of Peter Buck about the best new releases. Though Michael Stipe would never again ingest contemporary music to the extent he did between 1975 and 1977, there was still plenty to excite him, and Peter began putting aside those that he thought Michael would especially like.

Buck remembers his customer as being ''diffident'' if ''not real shy.'' Musically, the pair were on common ground. Both had been heavily influenced by the New York punk scene in general, and by Patti Smith in particular; and both had

after work, and as their tongues loosened and they traded musical opinions, they kept returning to the same issue: the possibility of forming a band together. Michael, still fresh from his experiences in St Louis, was determined to pursue the idea before he lost any enthusiasm; Peter had never found anyone suitable to pursue the idea with. The notion of teaming up together was not just attractive through the bottom of a glass; it felt good the next morning too.

■   ■   ■

T

The B-52's were an overnight sensation. No sooner had they formed their wacky dance band than they were living in New York under the wings of a major record company. Or so it seemed. Along the way, in the spring of 1978, they launched DB Records with 'Rock Lobster', a timeless cult classic and an inspiration to the region's music community.

"Of all the people I knew that played, and all the bands I'd seen in bars," recalls Pete Buck, "I never knew anyone from Georgia who had a record contract. When the B-52's put out

■ **Pylon at Tyrone's. Randy Bewley, Vanessa Briscoe, Michael Lachowski and Curtis Crowe.** (Terry Allen)

their first single on Danny Beard's label, it blew my mind: 'These guys have made a record and I can buy it!' Then when they got signed to Warner Brothers, it was unprecedented. Literally, there hadn't been anyone from Georgia get a record contract that wasn't beer and boogie and cowboy hats, ever.''

"They went to New York and became instant successes," recalls Curtis Crowe. "It looked so fun and easy, it was like, 'We can do this'. It seemed like a scream." Curtis and some fellow art students duly decided to form a band. Curtis would drum, Michael Lachowski play bass, Randy Bewley guitar and Vanessa Briscoe sing. They would call it Pylon.

"For us, it was a real art-related thing," says Michael. "We had done a lot of moving back and forth between different art disciplines. Doing art for us was an all-consuming thing, we didn't just do the work that was required at school, we did it all the time."

"Performance art" was Curtis' definition. For him, "The reason to be in a band was to go to these parties. The parties that the B-52's played at were so electric, so alive, we felt a real need to continue that excitement and energy."

But whereas the 'B's' had some degree of musical proficiency, Pylon were unschooled. From their début in March 1979 – at a party, naturally – it showed.

"I don't think they knew how to tune their instruments until they put out their first single," says Peter Buck. "I always liked in those days bands that would have one competent player and one guy who was learning, because it would push the band in different directions. Certainly with Pylon the only one who knew what he was doing was Curtis, so there was this real solid backbeat and there was all this chaotic noise and made-up words over the top.''

Pylon weren't the only new band in town. There was The Tone-Tones, whose lop-sided dance music saw them initially vaunted as Athens' next big thing; and The Method Actors, a more eclectic duo who debuted at a Halloween party Curtis Crowe held in '79 at his College Avenue apartment. None of them foresaw a future in music. "There was a sense of making art among these few bands," observes Jim Herbert, who socialised with them all. "I didn't see at that time any commercial possibility.'

The Tone-Tones dutifully split up within a few months. The Method Actors, however, would achieve cult status in Europe (and hence be away from Athens for long periods), while Pylon found themselves pulled forward in the B-52's' slipstream, releasing an acclaimed single on DB and becoming the darlings of New York. Unlike the B's before them, they chose to remain in Athens.

A decade after the initial 'clash of the rednecks and the hippies', that town was as uncomfortable with its contrasting cultures as ever. Despite its growing musical and artistic reputation, the University of Georgia was still most famous for its football team, the Georgia Bulldogs, and the macho behaviour that went with it.

Mark Cline, an art student who came to Athens in 1977, recalls he and fellow freshmen going to the wrong parties "where we'd get threatened with death – or worse! – because we were the weirdoes."

Peter Buck confirms that "All of us had those experiences. You wouldn't walk certain places at night, if you weren't with three or four people, 'cos they'd come pouring out of the frat houses and beat you up. I used to go in bars and get abused and get in fights because of the way we all looked. And it wasn't that weird: it was just very strange for some of these no-neck football players."

CHAPTER 2

The female scenesters suffered equal aggravation. At Reed Hall, the only co-ed dormitory on campus, some of them were taken to student court for playing 'punk music' – like Blondie's 'Heart of Glass' – too loud. The culprits, Sandi Phipps, Carol Levy, Cathy Russo and Linda Hopper, later joined by Kathleen O'Brien, went on to form an anti-sorority, DΦU [Defy You], in spite.

This antagonism between the old and the new was not confined to the streets and dorms. Sandi and Kathleen dee-jayed at WUOG, the college radio station, where their musical tastes – so harmless in hindsight – created a similar turmoil. So fierce was the battle between the jazz/folk crowd and the 'new wavers' that the station was taken off the air for three months to cool down.

The Athens nightclubs were equally reluctant to move away from what they perceived as majority taste. The Last Resort, for example, had a sign offering 'Folk, Jazz And Blues'. There was no mention of rock 'n' roll. Then in the spring of 1979 Tyrone's, a recently revamped club on Foundry Street not known for its adventurous booking policy, agreed to let The Tone-Tones play on an off night. The healthy turnout suggested that these local art bands could supply their own audience; gradually, Tyrone's booked them in.

Pylon made their debut on a Tuesday that July, as off peak a date as imaginable. "They were just floored by how many people showed up," says Michael Lachowski. "They just couldn't believe it." Though grateful for the paying customers, this young art crowd, so different from the traditional southerners who would booze the night away, weren't heavy drinkers. The owner suggested to Lachowski that they must all be on drugs "No," he replied. "If you're dancing, you don't drink."

Mark Cline isn't so sure. "Psychedelics have always been real big in this town," he says, from the days "in the late seventies (when) there really were no good clubs, so people would have parties and we'd all take lots of acid and go to these parties and dance."

Peter Buck somehow raised himself out of bed every morning after these binges to work at Wuxtry, and his boss Dan Wall took advantage of the quiet summer season to sublet a semi-converted Episcopal church on Oconee Street. He was immediately intrigued by the vast uncon-verted space he found behind the main bedroom, and being musically-minded, began cleaning it out as a possible performance space. Peter would frequently come around after work with a six-pack to jam on guitar while Dan played bass, and Michael Stipe too would occasionally stop by to sing along. With drummers in short supply, they used what Peter remembers as "a country Rod Stewart type" and Dan as a "redneck". His name was Tim, and he didn't last.

When Wall was called back to Atlanta to run the Wuxtry store there, he suggested Peter take over the lease, and made the same overture to Kathleen O'Brien. The pair knew each other from Atlanta, and agreed to share; with the rent a forbidding $350 a month, they scouted for other room-mates too. Michael Stipe jumped at the opportunity, Peter talked his brother Kenny into relocating, and a girl called Robin Bragg made it five. They took over the church in the autumn of 1979.

Although no one expected a life of tranquility in their new surroundings, they were all somewhat shocked at the reputation they inherited. "It had always been the party place," says Peter Buck. "So just because there were new tenants, didn't mean it wasn't. You'd come home at one in the morning and there'd be five people in the living room that you didn't know, drinking beer. Total strangers wandering into your house."

Sandi Phipps and the DΦU girls, having moved out of Reed Hall into a house on the Lexington Highway, regularly came by after classes. "There'd always be something going on there," recalls Sandi of the church's 24-hour party status. "People were aware of it for sure." Peter's extensive record collection dominated the front room and was the subject of much attention. Peter himself, recalls Sandy, was at the time "a cynical bad ass" who enjoyed raising hell. People enjoyed his company because "he was always ready for it, and fun at parties. It's always fun to go somewhere with someone when they cause trouble."

■ **Sandi Phipps.** (Sandra-Lee Phipps)

Kathleen O'Brien might have disagreed. On New Year's eve 1979, her attempts at civilised festivities at the church were dashed when Michael Stipe destroyed the Christmas decorations and Peter turned her elaborately prepared gastronomical spread into ammunition for a violent food fight. Furious at their behaviour, Kathleen engaged in a screaming argument with Michael's sisters, who then refused to talk to her for months to come.

It was all too much for Robin Bragg. "Her parents were thinking that higher education wasn't helping her," says Pete sardonically. "I just remember this real tense day when they came to move her out, and they seemed to blame her downfall on me and Michael." Robin was replaced by a girl called Pam Reynolds, whose extensive medicine cupboard ensured more around-the-clock visits than before. In the light of it all, the mail that still arrived for a previous occupant by the name of Purple Haze took on an acidic relevance.

Michael Stipe was evidently having the time of his life in his new surroundings. Though still outwardly shy, with none of Peter's excitability, he pursued his performing ambitions with a vengeance. For a while, he fronted a four-piece covers band called Gangster, taking the stage in an appropriate gangster's suit as he sang classic hit songs. The group was short-lived, and potentially embarrassing; he subsequently swore friends to keep their existence a secret.

In between the various partying, working, studying and performing, Peter and Michael were writing songs that their room-mate Kathleen thought were "wonderful". However, without a band, they looked unlikely to ever do anything with them. Kathleen performed with a group called The Wuoggerz whom no-one, least of all themselves, took seriously; it was more an extension of the friendship among the 'new wave' fans working at the radio station, whose call letters they named themselves after. Only their drummer came from outside WUOG. He was Bill Berry, whom Kathleen thought very handsome and had therefore befriended when he moved into dorms at Reed Hall on his arrival in Athens. Bill had a bass-playing friend, Mike Mills, and so, at yet another party, in January 1980, Kathleen introduced Bill to Peter. "You need a rhythm section," she told Peter; "you need a band," she said to Bill, and left them to it. Over a beer in the corner of some long-forgotten Athens front room, the pair agreed to get everyone together at the church.

To everyone who met them when they moved to Athens in January 1979, Bill Berry and Mike Mills were the closest of friends. No one had reason to assume it had ever been otherwise. Yet when the pair first met as ninth graders at high school in Macon, Georgia, it was animosity at first sight. Bill was enjoying the thrills of adolescence, "just starting to experiment with drugs and stuff," whereas Mike was a self-confessed 'goody-goody' who was everything Bill despised: "great student, got along with the teachers, didn't smoke cigarettes or smoke pot . . ." Communication between the pair was almost non-existent.

■ ■ ■

■ **Bill Berry, pre-R.E.M.** (Sandra-Lee Phipps)

REMARKS

Mike Mills, though born in Orange County, California, on December 17 1958, considered himself a local, having moved to Georgia as a baby. Bill Berry, when asked, would tell people he was born in Hibbing, Minnesota, "Bob Dylan's hometown." In fact, he was conceived in Hibbing and born, on July 31 1958, eighty miles away in Duluth, but it was more impressive to claim the same birthplace as the nation's unofficial Poet Laureate. (Ironically, the lie was unnecessary: Dylan too was born in Duluth, only moving to Hibbing as a child.) Bill and his extensive family lived all over the Great Lakes area – in Milwaukee, Wisconsin and Ohio – before the move south in the autumn of 1972. At the time, Bill felt the same horror at relocating in Georgia as would his future partner Michael Stipe, but when the Great Lake cities took the brunt of the 1970's recession, the entire family counted their blessings.

The Berrys arrived in Macon on the first day of 'busing', dropping Bill off at the local stop. By the time he got to see his new home that evening, he had been 'bused' from his prosperous new white neighborhood to a predominantly black school in that part of the city and back again. One of the few other white kids of his age was the 'goody-goody', Mike Mills.

Though they little knew it at the time, Berry and Mills were drifting together through music. For Mike Mills, his father an acclaimed dramatic tenor singer and his mother a singer, pianist and guitarist, musical ability was inbred. He studied the piano from an early age, and in high school joined the marching band, at first on sousaphone and then electric bass, an instrument at which he quickly excelled.

Bill Berry also grew up around music, his elder brothers and sisters purchasing all the latest hit records, his own tastes progressing fast; by the time he was eleven, he was a big Jefferson Airplane fan. Scoring high in a music aptitude test at school one day, he was encouraged to learn an instrument and chose the drums. So it came to be that he agreed to participate in an after school southern boogie jam in Macon, showing up at the bass player's house without enquiring who that might be.

It was, of course, Mike Mills, and Berry was inclined to storm out in disgust. As it was, he grudgingly decided to see the session through, and by the end of the day Mike Mills and Bill Berry were no longer enemies.

In fact, they formed a solid friendship and a rhythm section that began working together in every likely – and unlikely – scenario. There was the school marching band with its military uniforms, playing Led Zeppelin's 'Whole Lotta Love' to spur on the football team during games. There was the lounge trio led by their music teacher, playing country clubs and weddings dressed in suits and ties and earning a hefty $60 each a show as mere 17-year olds. And there were the rock groups, such as Shadowfax and the Back Door Band. Though they occasionally played originals, the demand was mostly for covers, be it in the one hand Freddie King or Meters hits, or in the other, the traditional southern boogie of The Doobie Brothers and Lynyrd Skynryd.

The pair would later look back and scoff at the music that dominated their teens, but at the time they knew no different. For Macon was the home of southern rock, where the Capricorn record label and Paragon booking agency handled the careers of legends like The Allman Brothers, Charlie Daniels and The Outlaws. On the occasion that Berry and Mills played that brand of rock at the Great Southeast Music Hall in Atlanta, 100 miles to the north, they could just as easily have considered themselves proud musical missionaries as the backwoods boys they were no doubt perceived as.

However, Atlanta was as far as the young rhythm section got; it became gradually apparent that special attributes were needed to break further into the southern music scene, and Bill and Mike – or the people they played with – just didn't have them. By now they had graduated from high school and, forsaking college, were sharing an apartment together. Mike Mills took employment at the local department store Sears; Bill Berry, still entertaining notions of a career in the music business, landed a job as 'gopher' at Paragon in the autumn of 1976.

In early 1977, as one of his many duties, he drove a fast-talking man by the name of Miles Copeland to a meeting with Paragon supremo Alex Hodges. Copeland was a Beirut-born American living in Britain, where he was booking the punk tours the more conservative agents wouldn't touch because of the movement's bad name. The excitement of punk had now gripped his two London-based younger brothers as well, Stewart, an accomplished drummer who was in a new band called The Police, and Ian, a booking agent. Miles looked out for them both, managing The Police and, when Hodges expressed his desire during their meeting to employ an aggressive young agent, convincingly recommending Ian.

Paragon, aware that southern rock could not rule for ever, wanted someone to bring in the best of the new international talent. Ian Copeland intended to do just that. He flew in to his new job, sat right down and played the company the punk music he said would change the world. The reaction from the hardened Southerners was one of horror.

"I was determined to get other people to listen to this stuff and see what I saw in it," recalls Ian. "And the more I was determined to do so, the less they did. In this whole town there was one person who started to like this music . . . Bill Berry."

Though everyone else in Macon quickly ostracised the 27-year-old agent, Berry and Mike Mills thought he was the coolest guy on earth. Mills even sold his bass amp to Ian, only to find himself using it more than ever.

"Bill and I got to be friends with him," Mike later recalled. "We'd go over to his house and he'd start playing us The Damned, Chelsea, The Ramones, The Dead Boys, The Sex Pistols, and I would put the headphones on and play his bass along with the records, going 'Wow! This is fun!' "

Copeland formed a part-time band with Bill and Mike at Paragon called The Frustrations, hoping to demonstrate to his agency partners the fun of playing the new basic music. He didn't succeed, any more than when he dragged them all along to the Sex Pistols show in Atlanta – leaving Berry behind working late on a hundred and one odd jobs.

The Sex Pistols split up within two weeks, and the Paragon staffers hoped Ian would now bring his tastes into line. Instead, he made plans to bring over The Police, and another of brother Miles' protégés, Squeeze. The latter he deliberately routed through Macon on their first American tour, spreading the word in true punk style by having Bill and Mike help him graffiti the town.

Most of this graffiti was still standing when, over Mexican dinner one night, Bill and Mike decided to enrol at the University of Georgia in Athens. Macon, they knew, was a trap – "If you weren't married, you weren't welcome," is Ian Copeland's lasting memory of it – and Athens was the

nearest escape route. Bill Berry, sufficiently intrigued after his apprenticeship at Paragon, intended becoming an entertainments lawyer, but took his drums with him anyway. Mike Mills bought his bass amp back from an Ian Copeland delighted to have influenced just two people in all his time in Macon.

Mike Mills and Bill Berry arrived in Athens in January 1979 and moved into college dorms. In May of that year, no one but its owner aware that the profits from Paragon were being siphoned off to prop up the ailing Capricorn record label, both companies collapsed. The era of southern rock was officially over.

■ ■ ■

When Michael Stipe and Peter Buck first set eyes on Bill Berry's proposed bass player, Mike Mills, they were horrified. "He was so drunk, he was hanging on to this bar and weaving," recalls Peter. "He couldn't stand up. Michael said, 'No way am I gonna' be in a band with him!' "

Stipe was more impressed by Bill Berry. "Michael said he liked my eyebrows," recalls the drummer of his dominant facial feature. "He claims to this day that's the reason he wanted us to get together!" Berry, meanwhile, considered Peter Buck "a little too cynical for his own good." Regardless of first impressions, they brought their equipment into the front room of the church – being the middle of winter, it too cold to rehearse on the altar – and decided to give it a try.

Peter Buck, the self-confessed amateur, was immediately daunted by Mike Mills' greater talent on the guitar. He offered to learn bass, but Mike and Bill were already a watertight rhythm section. He suggested trying a cheap electric organ that was in the apartment, but that left them still looking for a guitarist. So guitar it was, and much to his pleasure and surprise, "Bill actually liked my style. In Macon, everyone liked to solo all the time, and I think it was maybe the first time ever he played with someone who didn't immediately start going into the Gregg or Duane Allmann-isms. I think he found that refreshing."

Though he perhaps didn't realize it at the time, Buck was experimenting with the same chemistry that so impressed him about Pylon, bands with "one competent player and one guy who was learning". In this case, there were two of each, a remarkable collision of aesthetics.

Traditionally, American bands have been bred on a diet of technique and experience, and a belief in 'paying your dues' that often entails playing other people's songs for years. This was the classic approach that Mike Mills and Bill Berry had endured, an apprenticeship of endless covers bands running the whole gamut of musical styles through which they had developed an extraordinary understanding of each other.

But the punk movement, taking a leaf out of British rock in general, tended towards the untrained approach, best exemplified by the art school student who, having formed an idea in his head, simply picks up the instrument he feels best expresses that notion. Musical competence takes second place to originality and inspiration. This was Peter Buck and Michael Stipe's background, one where the rules – or lack of them – were learnt as much by reading the rock press as by playing on stage, and where musical training was never considered more important than musical intent.

With the common ground then also brought into the equation – Mills' and Berry's recent conversion to punk, Buck's love of rock 'n' roll tradition – it should have appeared obvious to any student of art or music that the newly-constituted group had explosive potential.

But with his lack of experience, only time would convince Peter Buck that the successful fusion of a group's disparate ingredients were not an everyday experience – although to his credit, he had shown extraordinary patience in waiting for the right band. "I just figured that you'd meet the right people, then you'd get in a band, then you'd make the good music, and people would come and see it," he says. "I didn't realize that most people spend their entire lives trying to find the right combination and it doesn't work. I didn't realize until about a year later that 'Gee, this is kind of special'. We never even tried anyone out. We were two separate camps. We basically walked in and said 'Hi, how are you doing?', picked up our instruments and two days later we were a band."

But at this point, they were a band with nothing to aim for. Kathleen, Sandi and the other girls would watch them practise during the afternoons, drinking and dancing and yelling encouragement. But too often the rehearsals would collapse into drunken binges, Mike Mills and Bill Berry collapsing on the sofa and subsequently skipping school the next day. So Kathleen O'Brien again played catalyst.

She was planning to hold an enormous 20th birthday party in the church on April 5, and asked them to perform at it as a birthday present.

Three weeks' frantic drunken rehearsal saw them establish two fistfuls of originals, and a few covers to pad them out. Mike and Bill brought in a song called 'Action' from their Macon days, while Bill also had a witty ode to his childhood television hero, 'Jacques Cousteau'. As with Peter and Michael's contributions – mostly 'love' songs with titles like 'Baby I', 'A Different Girl' and 'I Don't Want You Anymore' – they were primitive and simple, with a heavy sixties feel. The choice of covers was equally traditional: Johnny Kidd's 'Shakin' All Over', The Monkees' '(I'm Not Your) Stepping Stone', and a Buck-Stipe favourite, The Velvet's 'There She Goes Again'.

The daunting prospect of a public début failed to deter Michael and Peter, and two mutual friends, from taking a van to New York, where Pylon would be playing, over spring break. It would be a memorable introduction to the Big Apple for Stipe and Buck. Running out of money almost immediately, they ended up sleeping in the van (if sleep they did), eating rarely, drinking continuously, and washing only when the stench became unbearable.

But it was fun. They made friends with the performer Joe 'King' Carrasco, and thanks to Pylon, they got to attend a party of the New York élite, gorging on the free brownies and jelly beans and rejoicing in meeting the famed rock critic Lester Bangs at his most obnoxiously drunk. "You're a rotten cocksucker," were his only words to Peter Buck.

■   ■   ■

Kathleen O'Brien's birthday party would have been legendary even if none of the bands had ever played again. With her own radio show on WUOG and a job at Tyrone's, she knew as many people in town as Peter Buck, and the five kegs of beer, if not the three live bands all making their debut, were bound to guarantee a strong turnout. Yet no one had seriously expected 300–500 people to show up. Through the fog of time and the haze of whatever their poison was that particular night – qualudes were taken in abundance – those who attended best describe it as an 'event' without equal.

When the three groups had finished playing and their members, all still high on the excitement of their debut

■ **Kathleen O'Brien.** (Sandra-Lee Phipps)

performance, had resumed partying, people started coming forward to talk. Among them was Dennis Greenia, who lived next door to the church in a print shop with Rick 'The Printer'; they were both local catalysts who ran The Koffee Klub, a popular late night hang-out centrally located on Clayton Street. Greenia suggested that both the party's headliners and The Side Effects repeat their performances in two weeks time.

Mike Hobbs, who booked Tyrone's, was also impressed by what he saw. He had The Brains, an Atlanta band with connections to The Fans, coming into town soon and was looking for an opening act. If that last group could get a name together and would play for free, they could have the show.

Peter, Mike, Michael and Bill had been searching for a name for weeks. Now, with unexpected bookings to spur them on, they encouraged visitors to write suggestions in coloured chalk on the church walls. Among them were Twisted Kites – which some people believe was officially used at the first show – Cans Of Piss and Slut Bank. But the group wanted one that didn't mean anything, that left its connotations open to interpretation. R.E.M. ostensibly stood for Rapid Eye Movement – the condition during deep sleep when dreams are at their more prevalent – but it could also stand for anything else with those initials. R.E.M. it was.

At the Koffee Klub on April 19, the group again went on in the middle of the night. As the bars closed at midnight on Saturdays – Sundays in Athens being dry – and considering the venue's central location, it was perhaps no surprise that the police came crashing in halfway through R.E.M.'s official début and pulled the plug. Seeing people drinking beer, they stopped the show and subsequently charged Greenia for 'improper use of a business license'. Hoping to intimidate, they also took pictures of some of the 200 fun-lovers crammed into the tiny room. The night people posed readily, with great flamboyance.

Tyrone's on Tuesday May 5 was packed to the hilt. The Brains were one of Peter's favourite local bands, but R.E.M., by all accounts, charged through their set with such gusto and abandon that the headliners were left looking remarkably average. "It was generally acknowledged," Mike Mills later recalled, with the confidence bordering on arrogance that would prove an R.E.M. trademark, "that we blew them away."

Tyrone's proprietor Oliver Diamantstein noted that "when R.E.M. went off, most of the crowd left, and that told us something." He instructed Mike Hobbs to give them their own show as soon as possible.

R.E.M. headlined Tyrone's, on May 12, just one week later. "It was mind-boggling," says Peter Buck. "We got 350 people. Nobody got 350 people at Tyrone's. Pylon got 100. Everyone looked around and it was like 'I can't believe this'. We'd been together a month and a half and we were the biggest band in town."

For a few chaotic weeks in the late spring of 1980, the Oconee Street church was home to all of R.E.M., Bill Berry taking the place of a departing Pam Reynolds, and Mike Mills more often than not sleeping on the sofa.

But their lease was up in June, and the absentee landlord had heard enough about the incessant parties to want them out. After nine months' depraved existence, the occupants were equally ready for a change. Their deposit forfeited for damages, they left behind a host of memories and a squadron of sand-fleas. Michael, Mike and Peter subleased an apartment on Little Oconee Street for the summer – Peter paying the impoverished, unemployed Mills' rent – and Bill and Kathleen, who had by now entered into a turbulent personal relationship, moved in together around the corner. The church was duly rented out to another generation of students, who would come home late at night to a living room full of drunken strangers and ask themselves, 'Why us?'

■　■　■

The scorching heat of an Athens July summer's day greeted the freshmen students in town for 'orientation', an opportunity to familiarise themselves with the University and learn about the year that lay ahead. Like most of them, Bryan Cook was more interested in finding out whether Athens' nightlife opportunities were as multifarious as he had heard and, a keen music fan, followed suggestions to check out the students' fave band R.E.M. at Tyrone's. He paid his $1 and walked in on a group he'd always hoped existed.

"They were wearing these cool clothes," he recalls vividly. "Pete had a long, droopy ear-ring, and a pink silk shirt with big old collars on, and Michael was all colourful. They were doing 'Stepping Stone' and I just thought, 'This is the coolest thing in the world.'"

R.E.M. were moving fast. They had again upstaged The Brains when the two bands played the University's Memorial Hall on May 15, for which they received their first fee, a hefty $200. Now they were turning Tyrone's into their own private club.

The ease with which they commandeered Athens encouraged R.E.M. to look further afield. They made a low-key début in Atlanta at The Warehouse, and that same afternoon were videotaped by Dan Wall – who had also shot them at their Tyrone's début with the sound inadvertently shut off – practising in the back of the Wuxtry store there. That video remains the earliest – and least known or heard – group recording.

Then in July of 1980 Pylon, scheduled to play in North Carolina on their way to New York, cancelled when further prestigious dates in the big city came their way. Jefferson Holt, the young record store manager booking gigs in North Carolina as much to improve the local scene as his own

pocket, called The Method Actors as a replacement, who in turn recommended R.E.M. Holt booked the band on spec into The Station in Carrboro, a stone's throw from his Chapel Hill home, on Friday and Saturday July 18 and 19, and The Pier in Raleigh the following Monday. He expected the typical Athens art band; the one he got would change him for ever.

"It was the greatest thing I had seen in my life," he recalled five years later. "They had so much fun. They didn't seem to care about anything . . . They just got up there and had a great time. To me, it was how I imagined seeing The Who before they signed a record contract. It's what I think any rock band should strive for . . . a certain sense of chaos."

During their four days and nights in North Carolina, R.E.M. hardly slept, partying with Jefferson in their one motel room and taking pride that Kathleen O'Brien and Linda Hopper had driven up to see them. Buck, Mills and Stipe ended the 'tour' at The Pier on an empty dance floor while the 25-strong audience sang 'Gloria' massed on the stage.

At these early shows, one person grabbed the audience's attention with his theatrics and extrovert behaviour. It was the singer, Michael Stipe.

"He would get out there and shake and dance, like Little Richard or something," recalls Terry Allen, a young photographer on the Athens scene who worked with the group early on. "He had hair covering up his eyes, and he'd be shaking around, pulling the microphone up like Mick Jagger."

At The Station in Carrboro that first out-of-state show, a local rock critic, Fred Mills, was told by a regional musician that Stipe was 'the most pretentious Mick Jagger rip-off' he'd ever seen. Mills thought he was too self-conscious for

■ **Michael Stipe at Tyrone's, 1981.** (Terry Allen)

that, because "he would always look around. He wouldn't sing directly to you, the audience. I remember thinking he was more like Joe Cocker than Mick Jagger."

Mark Cline recalls Stipe "rocking, like Elvis, just shaking, and dancing around, and jumping", while Bryan Cook also remembers how, "He did the craziest dances. He'd go in all different directions, like a dervish, just spinning and jumping, his arms flailing . . ."

Scott Belville went to see his pupil one night at Tyrone's and was forced to do a double take. "He was hopping all over the place," he recalls. "And that was wild, because in class he generally was very quiet, very reserved." Fellow students familiar only with Stipe as an unassuming class mate "went there just to see him jump around."

It is hard to equate someone going through a self-confessed 'long and intense' period 'of extreme shyness' with the unreserved front man just described. Michael Stipe, however, would not be the first performer to appear invincible on the stage and intimidated off it: rock 'n' roll

has long been an acknowledged transformer of confidence for the emotionally shy. Certainly, from R.E.M.'s very first show, Stipe was bolstered by the genuine capability of the trio behind him and the obvious appreciation of the audience in front. The stage allowed Michael Stipe an opportunity to show off that he would never have the courage for on a one-to-one basis.

There was another Michael Stipe eager to be let loose in front of a crowd: the talented art student, who, taking a lead from the other Athens bands and his heroes from elsewhere, was working on the premise that art could be expressed in any form or medium, as equally on a stage as on canvas, as authentically through a microphone as through a lens.

Over a period of time he would develop this on-stage persona away from the shadows of other stars into something more mysterious and enigmatic, something closer to real art, and he would apply the same combination of inspiration, maturity and calculation to the lyrics. For

■ **R.E.M. at Tyrone's.** (Terry Allen)

■ The finale of R.E.M.'s first ever 'tour', July 21 1980, at The Pier, Raleigh, North Carolina. The audience is onstage, dancing; the group are on the dance floor, playing 'Gloria'. At right is Joe Thomas, a friend from Athens whom Peter Buck had just passed his guitar to. (Chris Seward)

now though, the words Michael Stipe sang related either to joyful quests for romance or typical teenage angst. Either way, they were embarrassingly juvenile and gave no indication of their writer's future literary credibility. Clearly enunciated choruses included the less-than-immortal lines "Baby I don't wanna hang around with you", "I just don't want you anymore", and "I'm running with a different girl"; the most profound they got were "These are dangerous times, I don't want to grow old."

The music of early R.E.M. was equally simplistic, both in form and substance. Largely due to Peter Buck's limited musical knowledge, they were all written around basic chord structures like A, D and E major. Buck's style of playing, however, was remarkably creative for someone so avowedly unaccomplished. Rather than strum chords, he would pick out arpeggios in the fashion immortalised by The Byrds, and throw in lots of the suspended fourths that had trademarked early Who songs. With the guitar such a dominant force in the three-instrument group, the entire sound thus took on a retro-sixties feel.

Yet despite their apparent shortcomings, the songs conveyed a charm and enthusiasm that has stood the test of time. An album recorded when they first started headlining Tyrone's – and there were certainly enough original songs for it – would have been a fine manic pop record. It simply would not have been the R.E.M. their audience has come to know.

In fact, the group did record their songs as soon as they realised they had potential, early on a performance day at Tyrone's on to a four-track recorder owned by the club. Of the eight numbers committed to tape – 'Dangerous Times', 'I Don't Want You Anymore', 'A Different Girl', 'Narrator (Jacques Cousteau)', 'Just A Touch', 'Baby I', 'Mystery To Me', and 'Permanent Vacation' – only one would make it on to an R.E.M. record, and that in far more dynamic style all of six years later. The others became gradually discarded would-be pop anthems.

■ ■ ■

In 1980, the talents that had been bubbling away for so long in Athens boiled over in a brief, tumultuous explosion of energy. It was a period of extraordinary creativity, an outpouring from which the town never looked back.

It was the year the Athens music community created their own club, The 40 Watt. Paul Scales, a scenester managing a sandwich shop on College Avenue, was offered use of its top floor as rehearsal space. He and Curtis Crowe instead turned the tiny room into a club, adopting the name of the Halloween party Crowe had held across the street.

"Not only was it a name," says Curtis. "It was an ethic. The ethic behind the 40 Watt Club was 'Something for Nothing'; if you can get out there and scrounge materials, you can put together something for nothing." The Side Effects opened the club on May 9 1980, and R.E.M. played there frequently for $1 admission, causing mayhem in a room Curtis describes as holding only "75 people – and you couldn't get another one in with a shoehorn." In some cases, the floor would vibrate so drastically under the weight of pounding feet that wooden pillars were eventually erected underneath. The thermometer never showed a temperature under 100°, and Michael Stipe could often be found manning the door.

It was also the year when Athens' previously small population of rock bands started breeding. The party at the church was the focal occasion – giving birth to triplets, so to speak – but it was not alone. Two months later, Love Tractor sprang up, an instrumentals-only group whose members Mark Cline, Mike Richmond, Kit Swartz and later Armistad Wellford were all known figures on the circuit. That Kit was also guitarist and singer with The Side Effects was not unusual in a music scene renowned for its incestuousness.

Socialising too reached a new zenith over this period. Michael Lachowski turned his answering machine into a "party hotline", on which he would leave details of the night's choice of events. He and Curtis Crowe lived in a house on Barber Street above Mark Cline, with Michael Stipe across from an empty lot that became known as Pylon Park. There they held parties throughout the summer, often with live music, always with a theme.

Barber Street became more than just a magnet for the musicians and artists in Athens; it became their own private neighbourhood, its two blocks at one time housing almost every member of R.E.M., Pylon, Love Tractor, The Method Actors and The Side Effects among others, along with their managers and close friends, and poets and painters. Over the decade, as more musicians than ever based themselves in Athens and some of the older ones bought their own houses, the locale expanded to become known as The Boulevard, including that street and Grady as well as Barber. To this day, all the members of R.E.M. own houses in that locality.

■　■　■

R.E.M. were instant stars in Athens. "That fall," says Bryan Cook, "was when they started owning the town. Whenever they played there'd be a traffic jam, and you couldn't park downtown. You'd see people walking, and they'd all be walking from wherever there was parking, down to Tyrone's."

But among their musical peer group R.E.M. were viewed with not a little disdain. Athens had put itself on the map by virtue of art-rock and intriguingly original dance-pop, and every time R.E.M. went into Tyrone's and struck up such familiar rock 'n' roll anthems as 'Hippy Hippy Shake', 'Route 66' and 'Rave On', they lowered the standards.

"At the time," says Terry Allen, "it was really uncool to be doing that, because it was almost like you were a bar band, just a cover band playing all the oldie hits."

"There was this kind of snobbery about bands who played covers," agrees Curtis Crowe. "The hipster scene was, 'They play covers, they're not truly hip.'"

"They were the odd band out on the scene," confirms Love Tractor's Mark Cline, "because all the other bands were art school bands, and here comes R.E.M. and they play sixties covers. They weren't real hipsters; they were kind of these outside rockers."

While these people stress that R.E.M.'s members were still welcome on a social level, there is no doubt that the band itself was ostracized by virtually all the local musicians. That they packed the clubs and appealed to all walks of people only emphasized their crassness. The *real* Athens music scene, said its leaders very loudly, had never needed to commercialize itself to please mainstream elements of the local populace; the sophisticates in New York had recognized its worth without their having to stoop so low.

■　**R.E.M. at Tyrone's, Athens 1981.** (Jay Thomas)

But R.E.M. were unruffled. They were merely having fun playing the music they liked; that it was instantly popular proved its merits. Admittedly, the traditional approach to their music gave them appeal in the mainstream, but they still had enough of the punk and art school ethic for the straights among those who attended Tyrone's to consider R.E.M. strange. It was the first evidence that the group's contrasting personalities allowed them to be all things to all people.

Still, playing covers was not the only reason for R.E.M.'s 'unhipness' among their supposed colleagues. Athens was acknowledged as an oasis in a musical desert; as such, its new bands saw no point playing the musically-prejudiced surrounding areas. R.E.M., however, so thoroughly *enjoyed* their first trip to North Carolina that they couldn't wait to repeat it. Rather than worry about the people who wouldn't like them, they instead focused on the few who would, and who would bring their friends next time.

It was a devotion to the work ethic that was to pay enormous dividends. By the end of their first year, R.E.M. had opened up hitherto unknown markets in Georgia, South Carolina and Tennessee. And in North Carolina, partly thanks to their new friend Jefferson Holt, they had built a following in Raleigh, Charlotte and Chapel Hill as well as regularly playing an odd little pizza restaurant in Greensboro called Friday's. Yet they still hadn't been to New York. The other bands in Athens thought R.E.M. were mad: who, they asked themselves, would want to slum it by playing the armpit of America when New York would treat you like kings?

The new-generation of 'post-punk' bands also steered away from the rough 'n' tumble bars of rural southern America because of the preposterously long sets they were expected to play: as many as three one-hour shows in the name of entertainment. Other groups saw themselves as outside all of that.

"We had no missionary zeal in trying to change people's minds," says Michael Lachowski of Pylon. "We only wanted to go where people were going to be already receptive." R.E.M. however, "loved to be on stage and be playing this stuff, and the crowd could tell. They could play to a more conservative crowd and get away with it, out of their sheer zeal, and ability to play long sets and covers."

In the process R.E.M. were undergoing the kind of intense group apprenticeship that can be compared to The Beatles' arduous days in Hamburg. Their enthusiasm enabled them to survive shows that would have enervated their uncompromising hometown friends. "We got together in front of people who'd never seen us, who didn't really give a shit and didn't know us," says Peter Buck. "You really hone the edge, having to prove yourself every night."

Athens regulars began to notice the increased absence from local parties and bars of the four men in R.E.M. They were on the road so much already – and earning so little money – that it was both difficult and pointless to pay the rent each month. Thus when they did come back to Athens, it would often be just to stay with girlfriends or on a friend's floor for a few days before heading out again. For a period during late 1980, Peter Buck even lived out of his huge old Buick, curling up in a sleeping bag in the trunk.

"I'd park it in front of people's houses that I knew," he says. "I used to shower at the dorms – I'd sneak in every day and

pretend I was a student." During this period of poverty and homelessness – his work at Wuxtry too irregular to constitute a living wage – Buck stored his clothes and records at the group's practice space. Other bands assumed it to be junk and removed almost everything while he was on tour, including the legendary pink silk shirt and many of his prized old records.

The other members of the group were also making decisions and suffering hardships. Neither Mike Mills nor Bill Berry had seen much reason to continue taking classes almost from the moment the group had formed. For Mills, life in an active rock 'n' roll band beat working at Sears in Macon, and that was enough. Berry, however, had gone to Athens with the noble intentions of becoming an entertainment attorney; if he was going to give up that ambition and quit school, it had to be for an equally attractive alternative.

More than anyone else in the group it was Bill Berry who picked up the reins when R.E.M. started. His ambition, business intuition and experience at Paragon had already landed him a job on the University's concert division, and now he applied these attributes to R.E.M.'s cause, hustling gigs at any and every little bar in the region. For a while he attempted to start The Athens Agency, whereby he would book out-of-town shows for the other local groups, but none of them expressed much interest in playing biker bars and pizzerias.

Berry then drew on his friendship from Macon with Ian Copeland to further R.E.M.'s cause. After the collapse of Paragon, Copeland had headed to New York to start his own F.B.I. Agency, a pun his brother Miles' burgeoning I.R.S. Records. There he could bring in the cream of the British talent and nurture the best of young America without having to answer to superiors. Berry sent Ian R.E.M.'s 'live' demo and some press cuttings to show their popularity. Copeland gave them a date with The Police in Atlanta on December 6 1980, Peter Buck's 24th birthday. Only eight months on from waking up with hangovers the afternoon after their first show, R.E.M. played in front of 4000 people at The Fox Theater in Atlanta, earning an encore and incurring the promoter's wrath by inviting the audience up on stage. How was Michael Stipe to know that the rules for a major theater were different than those for a tiny club?

By then Bill Berry had two drumming jobs, having readily agreed to fill in for Love Tractor when Kit Swartz decided

■ **Peter Buck at Tyrone's 1981.** (Jay Thomas)

that he preferred fronting The Side Effects. Berry enjoyed his new occupation so much that in the spring of '81 he told Love Tractor he was quitting R.E.M.. He no doubt meant it, but in actuality he used his dilemma to establish each group's commitment to going forward. R.E.M.'s being the far greater, he left Love Tractor instead. "He had to play devil's advocate a lot, which doesn't make you real popular," says Kathleen O'Brien. She praises Bill for being "totally instrumental in keeping R.E.M. intact" in those early days.

Berry became increasingly exasperated at having to hustle every minor gig and pull every major favour. Kathleen's continual motivation and encouragement – and her willingness to pay the phone bills – helped, but the group didn't want a female manager. Jefferson Holt, who was so infatuated with the Athens music scene that he moved there in October 1980 to open a new record shop, Foreign Legion, got involved instead. "He was the roadie at first," recalls Peter. "Then he took the door, then after a while he kept the money. Bill was going insane booking, so Jefferson started booking the band. After about a year, Jefferson was fulfilling all the jobs of a manager." Perhaps as a result, Foreign Legion lasted only two months before going out of business. The group, assured by Holt that this in no way reflected on his capabilities as a business manager, were happy to leave him to it.

But the most important development over that initial period was in the songwriting. In the summer of '80, Michael Stipe took a new approach with 'Gardening At Night', the lyrics of which were not only vague but largely indiscernible. He was rapidly moving away from clear enunciation towards a less guttural diction that paid only partial lip service to consonants and left the end of almost every line of verse unpronounced. He had discovered the power of mystery.

Mike Mills too was improving. He wrote a plea to Ingrid Schorr, a new girl in Athens who had been making a big impact on all the boys, begging her not to spend the summer of '80 in Maryland. 'Don't Go Back To Rockville', with its memorable chorus and frantic pacing, became an instant live favourite.

Mills' ability as a musician was also beginning to manifest itself. From the outset, he and Bill had supplied backing vocals that emphasised the group's sixties' influences. With Peter Buck's reluctance to take the melody on the guitar – although his arpeggio jangle was far more distinctive than most soloists with greater talent – Mills began to introduce it on the bass, supplementing the tradition of playing the chord's root note by supplying pertinent little incidentals at the top end of his instrument.

In the new year of 1981, R.E.M. wrote a song called 'Radio Free Europe' – ostensibly about the American propaganda station broadcast to the eastern bloc, but in reality almost completely unintelligible – that they recognised as a watershed in their short career. It was time to make a proper tape, and they headed to Atlanta to lay down the best of their own material. Completely naïve about studios, they allocated only six hours for eight songs; the hurried result was "flat and dull", according to Peter. Jefferson went so far as to say that it would do more harm than good to send it out, and suggested they try again, elsewhere.

He turned to his friend Peter Holsapple of North Carolina's leading band The dB's, who recommended another local boy, Mitch Easter. Mitch had set up a studio in his parents' garage in Winston-Salem and was looking for business. On April 13 1981, Jefferson called Easter to sound him out; R.E.M. drove up to North Carolina the following evening.

■ ■ ■

■ **At the UGA Art Department in Athens, which Michael was still attending as a student.** (Terry Allen)

■ **Michael Stipe at Tyrone's 1981.** (Jay Thomas)

Anyone who has heard him speak comments on the delightful twang to Mitch Easter's Southern accent, and everyone who has worked with him in the studio on his natural affinity for the recording process. Considering that Easter has been making rock 'n' roll since he was twelve, this is perhaps not surprising. During the late 1970's, he was in The Sneakers with Chris Stamey, and The H-Bombs with Peter Holsapple. When Stamey and Holsapple then formed The dB's Easter set his heart on owning a studio, selling his home in Chapel Hill and investing the profits in recording equipment. Like The dB's before him, he saw no future in North Carolina, but after a stint in New York that was even more frustrating, he returned south in 1980 when his parents offered him use of their garage. Winston-Salem was hardly on the cutting edge of music, but there were plenty of new bands in the region keen to find a studio not of the old Southern rock school.

R.E.M., though based 250 miles away, were a typical example. And when they turned up to Mitch's aptly-named Drive-In Studio that April evening, they were delighted to find it located in a sizeable house in the country, with dogs running loose and Mitch's mother supplying coffee and doughnuts. On April 15 Mitch engineered as the group raced through 'Radio Free Europe', 'Sitting Still' and the surf-styled instrumental 'White Tornado'. He was immediately impressed.

"I'd been recording some of the 'new wave' bands and I appreciated the spirit," he says. "However, a lot of them didn't live up to how they were live – they didn't have that many really good songs, And R.E.M. struck me as a real classic singles band."

Michael Stipe, much to Easter's amusement, insisted on singing in the furthest corner of the small studio where no one could see him, facing the wall. That the words were an almost total blur worried the engineer not one bit.

"I didn't care at all. Some songs that I really love and I hum in my head I've never known the words to. I like them just on the sound level. So I never worried about any kind of rule about that. I guess I had a really cavalier attitude about recording, and no concern at all for commercial stumbling blocks."

As a result, the group left Drive-In the following morning with a new ally and at long last, a decent demo tape. They were prepared to send it wherever need be to get attention but, eager to avoid appearing just another group of obsequious hopefuls on record company and journalistic desks, packaged it with colorful hand-designed insert cards and teasing instructions 'Do Not Open'. The ploy worked: when they at last journeyed to New York in June for a prestigious two night support slot with The Gang Of Four at The Ritz – another favour by Ian Copeland – they were met with a recommendation by critic Robert Christgau in the *Village Voice* that R.E.M. were "sending out a tape with lots of impressive first time songs on it."

■ ■ ■

In Atlanta Jonny Hibbert, a 27-year old law student and musician, was searching for the perfect act to launch his record label. His own band The Incredible Throbs had been in the process of splitting up when a couple of friends came forward with the money to put out a record; rather than stretch out his own flagging career, Hibbert suggested they search instead for a group on the way up. With little to get excited about in Atlanta, he turned to a student friend in Athens for ideas. Come see R.E.M., she said, and he was there the next time they played Tyrone's.

■ **Michael Stipe** (Carol Levy)

CHAPTER 4

"I wasn't particularly impressed with their musicianship or their artistry, or their stage presence either," he recalls of that first encounter. "There was no one element that I thought was really superlative. But it was the only band around at the time that created the same kind of crowd response and overall experience that I had always believed in as a performer. The fervour with which they approached their performances, and their sincerity, and the crowd's response to them, told me all I needed to know."

Hibbert duly approached R.E.M.. The group were attracted to the idea of a home-grown record label and, seeing that Hibbert was Holt's age and shared Mitch's musician's sympathies, felt they were taking another kindred spirit on board. When he offered to put them back in the studio to re-mix, and then release a 7" single in exchange for the publishing rights to 'Radio Free Europe' and 'Sitting Still', they jumped at the chance.

Later they brought Hibbert's contract to Bertis Downs, a local lawyer, friend, and obsessive fan, who was immediately appalled at the group's willingness to part with the potentially lucrative publishing rights. But by then it was too late: the copyright was with Hibbert's Dorothy Jane Music, and R.E.M. didn't want to start an argument. Downs shortened the deal to six months with no options; Hibbert kept the publishing.

On May 25, R.E.M. and Jonny Hibbert returned to the Drive-In to re-mix. When they left, Hibbert says it was with "the essence of a 45 rpm single . . . A record that was just full of energy, that made people want to dance, that was kind of fun, and kind of mysterious all at once. It had an innocence, yet a slightly sardonic angle to it too, which to me is almost the quintessential American pop single."

Mitch Easter, whose absurd dub mix of 'Radio Free Europe' created in his spare time had further endeared him to the group, wasn't so sure. "I told everybody 'I think it's worse, I think it's murkier than the original mix.'" He now volunteered to come up with a third, better alternative. He sent it down the following week.

When R.E.M. and Jonny Hibbert got together in Atlanta to make a decision, says Hibbert, "I had the attitude that if I was going to finance the manufacturing, distribution, the finished product of this single, it was to have my idea of what was airworthy." That meant his mix. The group favored Mitch's most recent offering. Peter Buck particularly, says Hibbert, became adamant about it. "I don't know whether it was lack of sleep, or what induced this unreasonable attitude on the part, particularly, of Peter. But . . . it was my decision. I said, 'This is my favourite mix, and the way I think the record will sell is if it has this mix'."

Further technical disagreements ensued over the mastering, and the initial test pressings were sent back as unacceptable. "I would be the first to declare the final product was not hi-fi," says Hibbert. "But it was I think as good as we could do with the budget."

Certainly the version of 'Radio Free Europe', backed with 'Sitting Still', that came out in late July 1981 on Hib-Tone Records lacked a vast amount of top end compared to Easter's mix that would eventually show up on the compilation 'Eponymous'. But that was only clear to those on the inside: judged against anything else it was an astonishing debut single. A feast of ringing guitar lines, melodic bass inflections and ethereal backing vocals set to a stomping four-square beat with a resoundingly simple chorus, 'Radio Free Europe' would have been merely a great power pop song but for its shrouded vocal lines that lent the track an indefinable edge. 'Sitting Still' was lighter, its guitars janglier, its vocals equally muffled. Overall, it was the definitive garage record of its era, from its release on a tiny new label run out of an Atlanta apartment, through its mid sixties, vaguely psychedelic sound, its almost deliberately obtuse sleeve featuring a blurred, indefinable Michael Stipe photo backed with an aerial shot of the group taken by Carol Levy, to its very recording in a suburban garage.

Both R.E.M. and Jonny Hibbert agreed early on to give away the entire first pressing of 1000 if necessary to create a

■ **Mitch Easter at his Drive-In Studio, North Carolina.**
(Melissa Manuel)

■ **R.E.M. from the same session used for the back of the 'Radio Free Europe' single by Carol Levy. Carol later died in a car crash; the song 'Camera' was largely inspired by her.** (Carol Levy)

reaction. The band, who saw the single mainly as an opportunity to improve their live bookings, spent hours sending copies to promoters up and down the country, and for good measure, to every magazine that mattered. The record impressed the club owners: by the end of 1981, R.E.M. had expanded their circuit to include far flung southern states like Florida and Texas, major eastern cities like New York and Washington D.C., and northern industrial towns like Minneapolis and Madison, Wisconsin.

In the meantime, Jonny Hibbert was fast slipping in R.E.M.'s favour. This was officially put down to problems unfortunately common with a new independent label: he could not afford a repress until he had the money back on those sold, and in the meantime, the stores went empty, if they stocked the record at all. But the major, unstated reason, was a personality clash. R.E.M. and Jefferson Holt had become a tight-knit unit with their own sense of vision; anyone who did not see things as they did was unwelcome.

Bertis Downs saw things as they did, and when they came to him concerned about other groups with their name, he suggested they put their entire house in order. "Someday you're gonna sell a million records and you have to be prepared," he told them, prompting much strained laughter. Even so, they agreed to follow his suggestions, and

were besieged with paperwork as Bertis, working for free, helped them set up their own publishing company, Night Garden Music, and their own corporation, R.E.M./Athens Ltd. In each case, recognising Jefferson Holt's total commitment to their cause, they cut him a piece of the action. He was now the official fifth member.

Jonny Hibbert claims he recognised a power struggle between himself and Holt as contributing to his estrangement from the band, saying that it was "possibly to their management's benefit, that there be some ill will, a gulf of malcontent between us . . . A manager's authority or grasp

■ **Bertis Downs IV, the loyal fan and fanatical lawyer who became R.E.M.'s co-manager along with Jefferson Holt.** (Sandra-Lee Phipps)

. R . E . M .

or control of a band is tenuous at best, and I think that everything that can be brought to bear to keep potential suitors, other interests and so forth away ... is to a manager's advantage."

This is arguably correct: Jefferson Holt has always been exceedingly protective about his charges, and Kathleen O'Brien says she too felt herself being quickly brushed aside from any managerial role when he entered the picture. Yet he was not unyielding. David Healey, an art student in Princeton, New Jersey, had been so captivated when the band played a party there that he too moved to Athens, in the summer of '81. Healey wanted to launch a record label, Dasht Hopes, with R.E.M., and unlike Hibbert, had the money to do so. Undaunted by their past experience – Healey was by now a close friend – the group readily agreed and began work on an EP.

Peter Buck describes the band that returned to the Drive-In for three days in October '81 on Healey's money as "confident enough to be quietly arrogant about our talents." As a result, on this session more than any past or to come, they followed no rules but their own. They set the bass amp up outside, and frequently the vocals too. "We

had this really almost flip attitude about recording," says Mitch Easter. "Or maybe it was me thinking, 'This isn't how you're meant to do it, so let's do it.' They appreciated that spirit as well."

Five songs were recorded: 'Ages Of You', '1,000,000', 'Gardening At Night', 'Carnival Of Sorts (Boxcars)' and 'Stumble'; for the last of these, Mitch indulged Peter's fantasy and inserted a backward guitar among the myriad of percussion effects. Easter, no mean guitar player himself, realised that in Peter Buck he was dealing with a distinctive talent.

"He played a lot of arpeggios, and he played all these kind of open chord positions with this combination of fretted strings and open strings, and I thought that was attractive. Having seen a lot of half-assed lead guitarists, it was interesting to see somebody who didn't try and be a lead guitarist, but just played this type of rhythm guitar that wasn't strumming either. It wasn't like he was playing anything that had never been heard before, but the fact that that was his sound all the time on the songs, and they were written around that, was pretty groovy."

■ **David Healey and Bill Berry in New York, April 1982.**
(Sandra-Lee Phipps)

As well as finding time to watch a firework show and see a band perform over those three days, they even put down a marathon "beat garbage dada thing" as Mitch describes it, called 'Jazz Lips'. It was an avant-garde collage of loops, feedback and effects topped off with Michael reading a beatnik sex story from an obscure 1960s skin magazine from which they took the title.

"We probably wasted a whole night doing it," says Mitch. "But we were having a great time. When you get involved in the process, and everyone's thinking alike, you don't even think about whether anyone else wants to hear it or not. You just go for it."

R.E.M.'s decision to entrust a record to David Healey reflected not so much a willingness to fall into the same traps as with Jonny Hibbert as an acceptance that there was hardly a record label in America they were suited for. In 1981, the only national underground movement, hard core punk, was avidly anti-commercial. When it came to searching out new trends to sell, the American majors were looking to the UK, from where The Police had proved themselves the first 'new wave' band to have mass appeal, from where Adam Ant looked set to do likewise, and from where 'Tainted Love' was on its way to becoming the big international hit of the year: what would become the so-called Second British Invasion was just beginning to gather speed. In this environment, R.E.M. recognised, no taste maker would pay much heed to an all-American garage band from Georgia.

The only U.S. company that seemed remotely suitable was I.R.S., whose roster included The Buzzcocks, The Cramps and The Go-Go's, and who had the power of A&M Records behind them. That they were owned by Ian Copeland's brother Miles gave R.E.M. a possible introduction, and so Bill Berry asked Ian to help. The agent explained he would gladly shop the band around all the record labels and was immediately told, No: R.E.M. only wanted to be on I.R.S.

"Well, that's easily done," Copeland assured Bill, suggesting he be remunerated for it later and giving Miles a copy of the original three-song demo. But when he stressed that the band were friends of his from Macon, Miles promptly wrote them off as being just that. Ian Copeland continued to help R.E.M. out with the occasional prestigious live show, but he couldn't deliver the record deal they wanted.

Mark Williams, a DJ in Atlanta and college radio rep for A&M (who distributed I.R.S.) now went in to bat for them. He sent a copy of 'Radio Free Europe' to the label's 23-year-old vice-president on the west coast, Jay Boberg (whom Ian Copeland also claims to have serviced). The reaction was favorable, and Williams encouraged him to see the band play when they would all be in New York for a college radio conference at the end of October. R.E.M.'s show at the Mudd Club there was not graced by Boberg's presence.

R.E.M. might not have meant anything to a west coast executive, but among New York's inner circle of rock critics and trend-setters, they were becoming young gods. The wheels set in motion by Christgau's comments in the *Voice* turned faster when their tape and single picked up favourable mentions in *New York Rocker* and *Soho News*. The latter was nothing short of ecstatic, imploring New Yorkers to see the group on their second visit to the city, at The Pilgrim Theater in the depths of the Lower East Side on September 16. When R.E.M. took the stage that night, it was to a warm welcome; when the PA broke down, and the group played instruments to fill the gap, the reaction was near hysteria.

"I remember everyone going wild," says Buck. "I guess usually when PAs break, everyone says, 'Well, we'll come back later'. We were used to playing bars, where fuck! You get paid, you gotta play."

One New York promoter particularly helpful to Athens groups was Jim Fouratt, who along with writer Tom Carson, stayed there for a week in late 1981. Both had received and admired 'Radio Free Europe' and were surprised to find R.E.M. so unpopular among the other Athens bands; Fouratt recalls being made to feel "really embarrassed" for liking the single. And when taken to see Linda Hopper and Lynda Stipe's band Oh OK support R.E.M. in Atlanta, their hosts even suggested leaving before the headliners. Fouratt insisted on staying and he and Carson were subsequently blown away by the band that night. But at a price: on the drive back to Athens, Fouratt recalls, "It was clear that I was not hip."

Fouratt was setting up a production company with a New York producer Kurt Monkacsi, and R.E.M. seemed an ideal first act to take on in the hope of signing them to a major record label. With their contacts at RCA – Kurt was engaged to the label's A&R manager Nancy Jeffries – they commandeered free studio time for the new year. Fouratt arranged it around the re-opening of his club Danceteria on Feb 3 and 4, which he asked R.E.M. to play. "I wanted them to open up because I thought it was very hip," he says. "I knew I would get critics."

By the time the group played the shows, their hip quota was even higher. 'Radio Free Europe' had featured in Robert Palmer's prestigious round-up of the Top Ten Singles Of The Year in the *New York Times*, and Tom Carson, still stunned by the show in Atlanta, had told the *Village Voice* readers that 'Radio Free Europe' was, "plain and simple, one of the few great American punk singles".

Why R.E.M. should have appeared so credible to trendsetters among New York's artistic community and yet not to those in their Athens hometown possibly had something to do with the 900 miles between them. Jim Herbert says that "Up north, they thought 'This is exotic', whereas down here, it may not have seemed quite so strange. Some people argue that we didn't quite get it because it didn't seem so unusual."

Neil McArthur, another member of the Athens art crowd who admits to viewing R.E.M. as "a traditional pop band" when they formed, verifies this. After moving to New York in the summer of '80, he returned south on a visit and, seeing R.E.M. live, "was just really struck by the southern glow they projected." New York critics saw R.E.M. as maybe the first post-punk band to emerge from the south and imbibe their sound with the region's atmosphere; Athens intellectuals saw that as being generic.

In New York on February 1 and 2, recording seven songs at RCA's studio, R.E.M. surprised producer Kurt Monkacsi with their professionalism. He wasn't to know they had come north straight from another two-day session at Drive-In, where they had put down a furiously-paced take of a song 'Wolves' among other new material. He was aware, however, that he and Jim Fouratt were unlikely to produce a deal overnight.

"RCA is notorious for not being timely in their decisions," says Monkacsi. "They've missed a lot of good chances because they're so big and it takes them so long to make up their own mind." Knowing this, R.E.M. had remained committed to working with David Healey despite the major label interest. It proved to be a shrewd move: although the

RCA demos caught the group at their most accessible, the company's head of A&R proved reluctant to make an offer. Thus the group went back to the Drive-In yet again in mid-February, and on March 9 sent Mitch Easter to Sterling Sound in New York to master a five-song EP. 'Ages Of You' they inexplicably dropped from the running order.

■   ■   ■

R.E.M. thought they had played enough no-hope little bars in their two-year existence to last a lifetime in hell. But The Beat Exchange just off Bourbon Street in New Orleans, where they were booked on March 12 1982, arguably beat them all, a junkie's haven with only a handful of patrons. In the middle of the show, the sound man simply disappeared, leaving the PA system to hiccup its way through the rest of the night. Afterwards, Michael Stipe sat in the tiny dressing room trying to laugh off their latest disaster when a smartly dressed young man walked up and introduced himself

"Hi, I'm Jay from I.R.S.," he announced.

"I was afraid of that," the singer replied.

■ Jay Boberg, President of I.R.S. Records.

At Mark Williams' suggestion, Jefferson Holt had mailed Jay Boberg a tape of the proposed EP 'Chronic Town'. The young label Vice-President who had enjoyed 'Radio Free Europe' but not acted upon it, was immediately won over by the new, less direct material. Despite his colleagues' skepticism, Boberg asked Holt to keep him informed of upcoming live dates. His girlfriend was attending university in New Orleans, and when he saw that R.E.M. were playing there it gave him the perfect opportunity to see both. Despite the junkies, despite the bad sound, he turned to his girlfriend three numbers in and told her 'I'm going to sign this band.'

Over lunch the next day, the two sides talked. Less than three years out of university – hell, he was younger than Peter Buck – Jay Boberg seemed to understand what the band did, and as importantly, didn't want to do. He was particularly intrigued by R.E.M.'s subtlety on tape.

"The thing that made me play the cassette again and again was that it kept getting better," he recalls. "It was not the kind of thing you listened to once or twice, casually, and said, 'Oh my God! This is tremendous!' It had a depth to it."

Boberg subsequently offered R.E.M. a deal. I.R.S. would release the EP R.E.M. had been working on, and then sign the band for five albums. The group would get good royalties against modest advances. "We agreed with that philosophy wholeheartedly," says Pete Buck, "because we figured the more we owed a record company, the more control they had over us."

Unknown to Holt and Downs, Boberg still required Miles Copeland's consent to sign the band, which he had not yet acquired. It was proof of Boberg's belief in R.E.M. that he wanted to present a *fait accompli* to his superior, yet had he confided in Miles earlier, he would have known how hard Ian Copeland too was trying to get a deal together. As it was, says Jay, Miles told him, 'If Ian will book them, you can sign them.'

Ian Copeland at this point was already in the unprecedented process of signing R.E.M. to F.B.I., with or without a record deal. The following that R.E.M. were building in every little town they played, not to mention the acclaim the New York élite was pouring down on them, was ample justification for such an honor; it is nonetheless unthinkable that any band would have enjoyed the same good fortune without the relationship that existed between Copeland and R.E.M.'s rhythm section. Ever since Mills and Berry had befriended him in Macon, Copeland had promised himself "If they were going to be in a band, I was going to be their agent."

Egos being as they are in the music business, there is continual dispute over who really got R.E.M. on to I.R.S. Jay Boberg says that "The deal had been done before I ever talked to Miles about it," while Ian Copeland insists "There's no question I was on to I.R.S. to please sign this band six months before Jay went to see them." Miles Copeland claims, incorrectly, that he agreed to sign the band as soon as he realised how serious his brother was,

and correctly, that "the initiating factor was F.B.I." So adamant was Ian Copeland that he had got R.E.M. where they wanted, he claimed his 'point' (a 1% royalty) on the whole deal that he had previously discussed. Boberg refused to pay it, and Bert Downs reduced it to a point on the first album alone, to be payable directly by the band.

Jim Fouratt and his proposed deal with RCA was left behind. The more Fouratt pressured Holt to put the band with a major label, the more he came to the conclusion that Bill Berry's loyalty to the Copelands was a bigger factor. Perhaps it was; most likely it was the band's eagerness to get on with the job here and now that swung the vote.

"We were in kind of a hurry at that point," admits Peter Buck. "We were writing songs like mad. We wanted to tour the country, we wanted to go overseas, we kind of realized this was possible. We were in a real creative space, and we just didn't want to sit around for two years waiting."

David Healey and his proposed record label was also cast aside. At the time he felt betrayed, and with no role to play in the R.E.M. organisation, left Athens almost immediately in dejection. In time however he would come to understand the group's decision and resume his friendship with them.

Jonny Hibbert, meanwhile, was totally out of the picture. Six months after 'Radio Free Europe's release, with 7000 copies sold, he lost all stake in R.E.M.'s continued recording career. But he did still own the publishing rights to the single. I.R.S. wanted to re-release the songs, and were as reluctant as R.E.M. themselves to let someone else make the money. Jay Boberg encouraged the group to buy themselves out of their relationship with Hibbert, making allowances for such among the advances.

Fortunately for them, Hibbert needed the cash. "I was real hurting for money," he admits. "And had certain pressures and crises in my life at the time. I didn't have anyone really close to me who understood the music business enough or had the discretionary income to help me through the problems." All he had were two songs by a group undoubtedly going places. He began touting the rights to them around publishing companies for an asking price of $10,000; he quoted an enquiring R.E.M. the same figure. Having signed the songs over to him for nothing a year previously, the group considered this tantamount to blackmail, and decided to call his bluff. They offered him $2000 not just for the publishing, but for the parts, the artwork, the rights to repress, everything to do with the single.

Hibbert could have legally kept the songs and in time become a wealthy man, as long as he paid the group's royalties every six months, but he says that "The band swore they would never ever release 'Radio Free Europe' and 'Sitting Still' on vinyl again if I didn't sell it to them," a threat Buck confirms.

Keen to continue Hib-Tone Records, Hibbert says he was encouraged by R.E.M. to believe that if he sold up, "it would present me to the music world, and artists in particular, as a fair player." In the meantime, he took on work as a roadie. Backstage at the Atlanta Omni one afternoon, Andy Slater, a former school friend of Peter Buck's, and now a hip young writer with *Rolling Stone*, approached him.

"He said 'Give the band what they want'," recalls Hibbert. " 'Give them a good deal, and get out of their hair. If you don't, your name's gonna be mud.' " Concerned at "the threat of a blackballing" and desperate for money, he sold up for $2000.

Jonny Hibbert's perception of his role with R.E.M. is as a gullible mister nice guy. "If I were to wish for an alternative course," he says seven years later, "then I really wish I'd just played hardball with them, period. I wish I'd given them what they have come to expect, what their preconception of a record label is. The difference was, I wasn't really a record label. I considered myself a fellow musician."

"An experience like that is good to learn in the negative," says Pete Buck. "We learned a lot of things: never ever again, we will never give up rights to our songs."

R.E.M. signed to I.R.S. Records on May 31 1982. That same day, they were back at the Drive-In recording a slower version of 'Wolves' and touching up the mixes. Their début EP, 'Chronic Town' was released on August 24 1982.

■ ■ ■

The period of intense activity leading up to their record deal with I.R.S. may have kept R.E.M. away from Athens for long periods at a time, but it also ensured they made the most of the town while they were there.

Just as Bill Berry left Love Tractor because of R.E.M.'s supposed single-minded determination, Michael Stipe sat down with Lee Self, guitarist with the band Vietnam, and formed another group. Stipe had already experimented with all-out noise with a short-lived outfit called Gaggle O. Sound, and now he went the whole way. Tanzplagen was the German word for dance torture, and Michael's choice of name was an apt one. The music was harsh and experimental, built around Lee Self's distorted guitar motifs, the untrained Neil McArthur's bass melodies, and the tumultuous drumming of Oh OK's Dave Pierce. Michael Stipe, in Lee Self's words, "had an old, gigantic, lumbering super-deluxe extra-big Farfisa organ with two keyboards and a big reverb unit which was kicked and shaken and dropped continuously during any given performance"; Stipe and Self both sang. The result was a glorious mess – what one onlooker recalls as "heavy metal dance disco before there was such a thing" – and the Athens art crowd loved it.

"One of the reasons we became friends and started working together," says Lee Self of his relationship with Stipe, "was that I was one of the few local musicians at the time to really respect and appreciate R.E.M." Certainly, Michael Stipe's standing among the art crowd was severely damaged by his continued participation in the much-derided R.E.M., and his role in Tanzplagen allowed him to regain some of that respect while indulging his artistic pretensions at the same time. Understanding this, R.E.M. encouraged his participation; in fact Tanzplagen had been due to support R.E.M. at Tyrone's a few days after the club mysteriously burnt down in January 1982.

Tanzplagen were a serious enough venture to undertake a tour of nearby States, and record a single – far less turbulent than the unlistenable live tape Michael Stipe would hand furtively to visiting New York critics – that included a duet between Michael and his sister Lynda. Its planned release on Dasht Hopes became exactly that when R.E.M. signed to I.R.S. and David Healey left town. Lee Self promptly moved to the natural habitat for his musical ambitions, Germany.

Seemingly at odds with its musical eclecticism and intellect, Athens during this era also experienced the formation of a private society for the male party animals in town. 'Mens Club' was a loose organisation that included virtually all of Athens' male musical entourage, among them Bill Berry and Mike Mills, the men in Pylon, and most of Love Tractor, Side Effects, and The Method Actors. Mens Club met at a maximum of 48 hours notice so as to enforce the spirit of spontaneity; in an attempt at formality, members were to dress in tuxedos, and to increase the air of sophistication, everyone would smoke cigars and drink spirits. These grand intentions rapidly degenerated, however, into feasts of beer and boiled peanuts.

"Everyone would intentionally be rude, and fart and burp, and tell stories," recalls Michael Lachowski. "Most of that was just posturing on a cartoonish level – telling a dirty joke and laughing super loud. We all knew as we did it that it was a joke. It was a reference to the concept of the Mens Club."

Attempts were nonetheless made to take this masculinity to extremes. "We always tried to get one girl there," recalls Mark Cline, "and she had to be topless and wait on everybody, and be in a really demeaning position." Curtis Crowe's future wife Diana volunteered – fully clothed – but "that didn't work out too well," says Curtis. "The trouble with her was we all knew her, and so we couldn't really be demeaning to her."

Mens Club therefore became exactly that, an exclusive male organisation. "There were some true social exchanges that could never have happened in mixed company," recalls Lachowski. "And that's where that specialness came in: there was this kind of esprit de corps that evolved. It evolved its own charge."

When Neil McArthur returned to Athens in October 1981 and heard of these gatherings, he considered it an appropriate welcome back gesture on his part to host the next one. He had no idea what he had let himself in for. The Athens

women decided it was time to put an end to the men's chauvinism and decided to gatecrash – even though they themselves had an equally close bonding – led as usual by Sandi Phipps and Kathleen O'Brien.

"I guess they didn't understand that to tamper with our moods at that point was a real uncool thing to do," says Michael Lachowski. As soon as the girls walked in, they were seized upon and fiercely ejected. Kathleen in particular needed five men to control her as she twisted like a wildcat. It was an ugly scene.

"We thought they were going to regroup," recalls Neil, "and so, in our drunken stupor, we thought we had to barricade the doors. People started picking up every piece of furniture I had in my living room and throwing it against my front door – which included sofas and telephones and lamps and one glass table which got shattered."

The destruction at Neil McArthur's apartment convinced Bill Berry and Mike Mills, who were now living together on Barber Street, that they would be the perfect hosts for the next Mens Club. They were. The night started with the building of a 'Moon Pyramid' of male buttocks – of which photos were taken – and ended with a paralytic Bill Berry standing on the living room table with his favourite golf club, crying 'Fore!' and launching every single piece of glass in the house into the fireplace while his companions ducked for cover in hysterics. Legend has it that it took days to remove all the splinters of glass from his face.

■　■　■

■　**The Barber Street home of Bill Berry and Mike Mills, location for many a legendary party.** (Sandra-Lee Phipps)

(Sandra-Lee Phipps)

Essentially, the group that released 'Chronic Town' was still a garage band. R.E.M.'s live show had sacrificed none of its gritty core in accommodating the new material, and as people, they remained down-to-earth rock 'n' roll fans on a constant quest for the next good time. But on record, they had turned into something else entirely. With 'Chronic Town', R.E.M. learned how to isolate themselves from the pack by becoming an enigma.

Mitch Easter's production was the first integral factor in the public's perception of R.E.M., his carefully layered tracks and array of effects staving off an otherwise overt sixties obsession without bringing the result too closely into line with its contemporaries.

Michael Stipe's vocals were another key element. Swathed in blankets of fog, their haunted quality was like none heard in years. Unable to pick out more than but a few key phrases, observers assumed they were hearing a vocal buried in reverb or drowned in the mix, something Easter vehemently denies.

"A lot of people literally ask me what the box was. But there's nothing like that going on. It was absolutely standard vocal processing you do on anybody. I've read so many people talking about Michael's vocals being buried, but they're not. You go back and listen to 'Wolves' and it's as loud as a Tom Jones record. He's out front, but he just sounds like that."

The third ingredient in R.E.M.'s recipe for intrigue was packaging. Neither the glum gargoyle on the front sleeve, the band's bemused expressions on the back, or the 'Chronic Town'/'Poster Torn' subtitles for sides one and two gave the EP as much mystery as the song titles themselves. They were, without doubt, wilfully obscure: adding the word 'Lower' to the title of 'Wolves', for example, was a master

stroke of perversity, giving an ostensibly clear title a completely indirect meaning. 'Wolves, *Lower*'?, people asked. '1,000,000' *what*? 'Stumble' *where*? How *many* 'Carnival of Sorts'? And as for 'Gardening At Night'...

"Some people think it's about my father; some people think it's about drugs; and some people think it's about gardening at night," said Michael Stipe to this last, frequently-asked question. "It's all of them." Or none, as the case may have been. He readily admitted that after the 'simple pictures' of his early songwords, he had "started experimenting with lyrics that didn't make exact linear sense."

"Part of it," explained Peter Buck on Michael's behalf, "is that as we went along we realized that we didn't want to be a straight narrative band that has stories in our songs that began and ended. You can put meaning in there – you can write a song about something without ever really referring to what you're writing about – by using evocative phrases, by association of words that you wouldn't normally associate, by repetition, by the power of the music itself and the melodies. You can get the feeling from that experience without ever actually referring to the experience itself."

Bill Berry too caught the mystery bug. A Chronic Town, he said when asked, "is a city in the state of mind".

But the more subtleties and riddles that ordained R.E.M. on record, the harder they were going to be to break commercially. Within the small ranks of the I.R.S. office, only Jay Boberg was visibly excited about the new signing. His counterparts clung to the same negative opinions they had voiced when first played a tape several months previous. The only one way to build R.E.M. was on a grass roots level, market by market, and so, for the release of

■ **Michael Stipe outside the Iroquois Hotel in New York, April 1982.** (Sandra-Lee Phipps)

'Chronic Town', Boberg brought them out to their biggest untapped market, the west coast, to put the personal approach into practice.

Spending an entire month in California, R.E.M. gradually turned a lukewarm reception into another firm fan base. Their LA début at the Music Machine was ill-attended, but they succeeded in winning over the team at I.R.S., and even made a video for 'Wolves, Lower' at Club Lingerie in Los Angeles, an inexpensive, one-camera shot that they hated but that nevertheless got some exposure. They spent a few days in San Francisco, opened for The English Beat and played some dates on their way back east with their heroes The Gang Of Four. And in Los Angeles, they found other groups like Dream Syndicate and Three O'Clock sharing their love for psychedelia and The Velvet Underground. College radio was playing them, and the press wanted to write about them. Maybe they would just stay on the road for ever.

■　■　■

At the beginning of 1989, talking to *Rolling Stone*, Michael Stipe reflected on the R.E.M. that was once permanently on tour. "If there's an extension of 'On The Road' and that whole Kerouacian . . ." – laughing at the word and continuing – "If there's an extension of that, probably forming a rock band and touring is the closest you could get."

There was a time, from 1980 through 1982, when R.E.M. really did live on the road: four young men and a devoted manager, in the prime of life, travelling from town to town across America in a 1975 green Dodge van bought with the profits from a couple of well-attended home town shows, playing a backwoods circuit no rock band had yet discovered. Permanently broke, often without a home to return to – legend has it that when they were unable to meet the rent, they simply padlocked their doors and went out on the road to earn it – frequently playing to a handful of disinterested drunkards, testing each other's nerves . . . such circumstances should split even the most determined of rock 'n' roll bands. And when they don't, when that band keeps coming back for more of the same arduous lifestyle, when they actually look forward to the next gruelling trip with the anticipation of a five-year old on an outing to the country, then it's obvious they have a fire burning of such intensity that nothing can stop them.

There were occasions when someone wanted to quit, certainly. When personality clashes reached a head, or a particular show was such a complete waste of time that someone would say, That's it, I've had enough. But each time, the injured party came to realize that they had come too far to turn back now, and that the magic of R.E.M. was the product of the four individuals combined; if one of them bailed out, the ship would probably sink as a result.

The other Athens bands could only look on with a mixture of befuddlement and admiration. "It's the standard business formula for success," observed Curtis Crowe enviously in 1989. "Have an idea and go for it morning, noon and night. Just do it with absolutely relentless desire." Pylon never had that sense of drive, and unwilling to confront the business side of the music business, ground to a halt in 1983.

Love Tractor too, were not prepared to endure the hardships. Despite R.E.M.'s entreaties to join them on their new found circuit, they had college to attend to and jobs to keep. Weekends in Georgia and the occasional trip to New York would suffice for their live schedule.

Similarly, Jonny Hibbert, for all his disappointment with the group's treatment of him, recognizes what made them ever have anything to fight over. "The biggest reason that record ['Radio Free Europe'] and this band was a big success was because of the band getting in this drafty old green Dodge van that leaked exhaust up into the cab, and travelling from here to Timbuktu and back, and living like a young starving band on the road. Which meant sleeping on floors, sleeping in the truck, night after night, mile after mile. They would be gone for two and three weeks at a time. They get the credit."

"I had that kind of romantic view of going on the road with a rock 'n' roll band," says Peter Buck, who has always enjoyed a reputation as the R.E.M. insomniac. "What does a band do on tour? You drink all the time and meet girls, and don't sleep. I could go a week without sleep in those days, just about. I don't think I touched a bed in two months sometimes; I'd sleep sitting up in the van on the way to the show. Or usually, we'd play, go to a party, drink, steal food from the fridge and then at around four in the morning, we'd go 'OK, time to go on to the next town'. We'd drive into

■ **The first photo session after signing to I.R.S. in May 1982. Michael Stipe complained that Mike Mills always looked like a "laboratory animal" in photographs. Mills would later choose to keep his glasses on during sessions.** (Sandra-Lee Phipps)

the next town, and arrive there at noon, park behind the club and sleep until five."

In 1981 Hüsker Dü burst onto the scene with an album called 'Land Speed Record', a direct reference to their ingestion of amphetamines, and though R.E.M. have tended to be coy about such matters, a group driving thousands of miles in extreme discomfort with little chance for sleep is unlikely to get by on natural adrenalin alone. Such is the reality of life in a rock 'n' roll band. Certainly, despite the heavy partying – and on that personalized circuit of small clubs, someone would always offer up their apartment for a post-gig soirée – they were consistently capable of putting in energetic shows night after night, Buck in particular careering around the stage in a frenzy like a spinning top gone wild.

From the outset, R.E.M. saw a circuit opening among the increasing number of 'new wave nights' being promoted by the assorted bars and nightclubs around the south central area. They were usually on weekdays, the weekend reserved for the southern rock acts and their hard-drinking audience or for the disco crowd, depending on the location. The inane catch-all term paid off for clubs like The Pier in Raleigh, North Carolina, whose 'New Wave Mondays' were able to attract prestigious names looking for a date on their way through to bigger towns. Local audiences slowly turned on to the fact that it just might be worth going out to these events.

As R.E.M. progressed on that circuit of backroom bars, night clubs and college parties, they noticed the same names criss-crossing paths with them: Black Flag and The Minutemen from California, The Replacements and Hüsker Dü from Minneapolis, The Neats and The Lyres from Boston . . . As they got to know these bands, and many more, by turning out for each other's shows, even sharing the same stage on occasions, they got to form friendships and a loose affiliation of kindred spirits determined to make a change.

R.E.M.'s following grew steadily, but there was always a badly advertised or ill-arranged show to bring them back down to earth. In April 1982, living on the road to make the most of 'Radio Free Europe's surprising success, they followed up a couple of prestigious New York dates with a midweek trip to Detroit on a night that the venue rarely even opened.

"There were five people there who happened to be driving by who were all on mescaline," recalls Peter Buck. "They enjoyed the hell out of it, they all had a great time. They asked us for an encore, and we came back out and said 'Listen, this is ridiculous, there's as many of us as there are of you. We'll just take you to dinner.' We made $300 that night, so we took them to this Greek restaurant."

Such occasions did nothing to dampen R.E.M.'s collective spirit. "I remember playing at The Antenna Club in Memphis," says Buck, "and we were playing really well. But there were only about eight people there, and two of them were this old wino man and woman, and they were dancing in front of us, like waltzing, and slobbering on each other, and groping. Some people would think that's humiliating, but I thought 'We're playing really well; I don't care if there's old winos having a good time and six people at the bar.' Even if you only had three people, those three people would be saying 'God, they're pretty good'."

On signing to I.R.S., and with the backing of F.B.I., R.E.M. might have assumed those days were over. Their two most sublime shows were yet to occur.

Driving out to the west coast in August 1982 for that first month in California involved a 1400-mile, week-long void between Austin and San Diego. With no 'new wave Mondays' or progressive pizza restaurants in this neck of the woods, F.B.I. could come up with just one date, in Albuquerque, New Mexico. The band drove into town only to find they were opening for a Hot Legs contest.

"These professional strippers were coming and doing obscene dances," says Peter Buck, whose memory of the club is a drunken audience a thousand strong chanting for 'tits and ass'. The promoter looked at the oddly-dressed bunch of Athens ex-college boys, at his raucous crowd of cowboys, and back again.

If you go on before these naked women, he told the group, I'm worried that these guys are going to kill you. Better I pay you your $500 and you go on your way. A flabbergasted R.E.M. took the cash and hurried off on the next 700 miles of their journey before the promoter could change his mind.

More than a year later, with their debut album causing a noticeable stir and a considerable following in much of America, F.B.I. booked them and Mitch Easter's new group Let's Active into an Air Force Base in Wichita Falls, Texas. Michael Stipe's sense of déjà vu as they drove up to a compound all too familiar from his childhood was enforced when they took the stage to face a sea of rednecks with crewcuts. The music that was winning them critical acclaim across America did not score points with the men of the USAF.

"There were oranges flying out of the audience," recalls Peter Buck. "They were passing notes: 'If you play one more song like this, you DIE, faggots!'"

"These guys would not get really violent, because they'd be arrested by the MPs," said Michael Stipe a year later. "But they had this mock violence and mock threatening and that was more frustrating to me than just having them come up and smash our heads in."

Not even the group's repertoire of Rolling Stones songs could appease a crowd hungry for ZZ Top and Van Halen. Finally, Bill Berry stormed offstage, leaving Sara Romweber from Let's Active to take his place and finish the show to thunderous booing.

"I remember Peter demanding the band break up over that, (because) it was so unprofessional," recalls Mitch Easter of Bill's abrupt departure. "It was actually sort of funny. Everybody got mad with everybody, and everybody was gonna quit, and so and so wasn't ever going to play in a band with so and so again. There were varying degrees of temper within the band. It takes a long time for it to sink in just why you have to put all of that aside."

A night straight out of the celebrated rock 'n' roll satire

documentary 'This Is Spinal Tap', the events of Wichita Falls were matched only by the drive from New Jersey to Michigan for the afore-mentioned ill-attended Detroit show.

High up in the mountains of Pennsylvania in the still of night, Bill and Peter pull the van over at the Howard Johnsons to get coffee and relieve themselves. They ask if anyone needs anything, but are greeted by silence. Everyone is asleep.

Almost a full hour after resuming the long journey north, Mike Mills wakes up. He asks what happed to Jefferson. Peter tells him he's asleep in the back. Mike insists he's not. Michael Stipe wakes up and confirms it: Jefferson is not there. Realization sinks in. Their manager had got out at the service stop without telling anyone, and the group had driven off without him.

With Jefferson carrying the tour float, they must turn around. But on this winding mountain road with a fence running along the central reservation, there is nowhere to do so. It's a further twenty miles before they find an exit, another hour and a half before they return to the Howard Johnsons. There, a despondent Jefferson Holt sits by the kerbside, waiting patiently. No one says a word as he gets back in and the group resume their journey, almost 200 miles and two and a half hours behind schedule.

Years later, travelling in luxury coaches with bunk beds, VCRs and stereos, to towns where their equipment would already be set up and hotels await them, where the audience would know what was in store and the strippers were confined to the local go-go bars, they would look back on those days in the faithful Dodge van, on the sleepless nights, the endless drinking, the disasters, the triumphs and the pocket-sized crowds they knew by name, and think, We wouldn't have missed it for the world.

■ **In full swing at Tyrone's, R.E.M.'s favorite haunt, during 1981. Michael Stipe was so quiet and reserved at art school that fellow students went to Tyrone's "just to see him jump around."** (Terry Allen)

■ ■ ■

'Chronic Town' **exceeded** **expectations,** staying on the top five of the college radio charts for three months, and notching up 20,000 sales by the end of the year. October saw a *Rolling Stone* story by Buck's ex-college associate, Andy Slater, and in February, the *Village Voice's* Pazz & Jop Poll rated 'Chronic Town' second best EP of 1982, T-Bone Burnett taking the gold medal and The Dream Syndicate the bronze.

For now, however, the issue at hand was making the album. Jay Boberg suggested they expand their options and try recording with a then unknown producer Stephen Hague. They went into a 24-track studio in Atlanta with him to work on 'Catapult'.

"I just thought 'This is exactly what I would expect'," says Mitch Easter of the move. "Because no doubt I.R.S. thought I was some Southern good buddy sound man friend of theirs who's not qualified to make a real record for a real record company. They'd never heard of me before, so understandably they'd go for somebody they had heard of. I just don't think that the idea of making a record down here sounded very wise to them."

Jay Boberg totally refutes this opinion – "By that point we'd already talked about signing Mitch Easter" (Let's Active joined the I.R.S. roster in '83) – and stresses that it was just "an idea". Peter Buck says the group's attitude at the time was "We'll try anything," but that they stressed to I.R.S. they would sooner work with Easter.

Once in the studio, they were subjected to the rigidity of performance and lack of artistic control so familiar for newly-signed acts. Recording to a metronomic 'click track', they played 'Catapult' so often that they lost the feel for its emotion, after which Hague took the tapes to a Boston studio and added synthesizer overdubs that mortified the band. "It was just not a very pleasant experience," says Buck.

It had already been agreed that Mitch Easter would have an equal shot at producing a new song. His own 16-track Drive-In not up to standards, Reflection Studios in nearby Charlotte was the obvious alternative, but, Mitch says, "I didn't really have the confidence in those days to walk into a studio like Mr Big Producer."

He therefore asked Don Dixon, whom he had known since high school, to co-produce. Dixon was five years his senior,

■ **Don Dixon at the Drive-In Studio.** (Godfrey Cheshire)

but like Mitch was a North Carolinian musician – his group Arrogance were the state's biggest resident band – becoming increasingly adept behind the mixing desk. He had helped out with the mix for 'Wolves', was stunned by R.E.M.'s potential when taken to see them, and felt the same need as Mitch to protect the group from the often dictatorial music industry.

"I think we understood things about the band the record company didn't," says Dixon. "We understood that the combination of their limitations as musicians was a big part of the sound, so you don't just throw those out, and go in and put a Curtis Mayfield arrangement on it. It was important for them to understand that we very much liked what they were doing, and we wanted to preserve that over the record company's dead body."

Although the group were, according to Dixon, undergoing "a real crisis of confidence" after their experience with Hague, they emerged from their two days at Reflection at the beginning of 1983 with a beautiful rendition of the song 'Pilgrimage', enhanced by layers of Gothic background vocals. Jay Boberg, recognizing how well R.E.M. worked with their Southern partners, gave them the go-ahead to make the album.

Reflection's isolation allowed the group to record without the big city pressures of New York, LA or even Atlanta. The studio received most of its bookings from religious organisations – from the notorious PTL television ministry to less materialistic black gospel groups – and there is no question that R.E.M. inherited some of that spirituality in their search for a memorable début album. 'Chronic Town' had opened up a myriad of possibilities they now wanted to explore, and, having begun to describe themselves as 'folk rock', it was obvious they wanted to capture an entirely different R.E.M. on record from the one that gave such hectic live shows.

To this end, acoustic guitars became the rule rather than the exception – backing tracks often featuring Buck, Mills, Berry and either Easter or Dixon all strumming the same chords together – and ideas sprang from all sides. For the new version of 'Radio Free Europe', they re-routed the studio's inherent hum through Mike Mills' bass for a futuristic intro; on 'We Walk', they amplified and altered the sound of Bill Berry playing pool underneath them; with 'Perfect Circle' they incorporated backward guitars and a childlike pattern played on both a grand and an out-of-tune upright piano; on 'Talk About The Passion' they brought in a 'cellist. 'Sitting Still', meanwhile, was left almost intact from the B-side of the Hib-Tone single.

Michael Stipe again recorded out of view, in a stairway off the control room leading downstairs. His style of vocal no more worried Dixon than Easter before him. "Michael had a delivery whereby you could solo the vocal and still have no idea what he was saying," says Dixon. "It's because he liked the way things sounded as much as he cared about what he was trying to say." To this end he was helped enormously by Mike Mills' backing vocals that eschewed traditional harmonies, interjecting to the extent of becoming secondary melodies.

Although there were occasions when Easter and Dixon's suggestions would provoke instant rejections from a group still worried about losing their essence to hi-tech production values, the month long session is remembered by all as an untroubled collaboration. "Every time the tape would roll, it was pleasurable to hear it," says Mitch Easter.

"Mitch and Don," says Peter Buck, "thought their job was to make us make a good record, and not worry about selling records for record companies. So they were like partners in crime with us; they were protecting us from outside influences or financial influences that might come into it. So they were gambling in their own way too. For both of them, it was their first major label record. It was like, 'What if everyone hates it?' but they were willing to go that distance for us."

Such was the smoothness of the sessions that a night was dedicated to recording other material live onto two-track. Some were originals already in the group's set – 'That Beat', 'Pretty Persuasion' and 'All The Right Friends', a less blatant title than its previous 'I Don't Want You Anymore' – but they also recorded some covers at Peter's behest, the group's archivist already thinking ahead to future B-sides. Two of these recordings would eventually end up on vinyl, Archie Bell And The Drells' 'Tighten Up', on which Easter played xylophone, and The Velvet Underground's 'There She Goes Again', on which the propulsion of Buck and Easter's dual acoustic guitars and the superb vocal harmonies made for an honourable rendition.

"When you've just got through something, you don't really know what you've got there," says Mitch Easter. When R.E.M. finished 'Murmur' – an apt title indicative of tentative first steps, whispered suggestions and also, as the group were wont to say, 'one of the seven easiest words to say in the English Language' – they were excited but nervous.

"I remember thinking 'God, I can't wait until everyone hears this'," says Peter Buck. "Because it was different: it didn't sound like our other records, it didn't sound like us live, and it didn't sound like anything else that was coming out. It was the first time I thought all the songs were really strong; some of them were so on the money I was real happy. I didn't know if anyone else was gonna like it or not. In fact, we played it for our friends and they were all saying 'God, that's weird, it doesn't sound like you at all.'"

"I felt like we'd done a real cool thing," says Dixon of his and Easter's efforts. "But we figured it would be like a lot of other good records we'd made: it would sell a few thousand, cool people would like it and most people would never get to hear it."

They were wrong.

■   ■   ■

Only rarely does a début album succeed in capturing a group on the brink of becoming a shattering new talent, one that has already honed its craft into a distinct sound, that has the ability to capture that identity in the studio, and the purpose of mind to retain control while doing so. 'Murmur' is such an album.

What makes it all the more special is that it was recognized as such. For 'Murmur' was not an instant classic. On first exposure, the uninitiated would be likely only to agree that there was promise lurking inside. But over repeated playing a web of intrigue wove its way inside the listener's conscience, naïve melodies and snapshot phrases gradually permeating the pleasuredome. Only then was its beauty apparent.

Fortunately for R.E.M., when 'Murmur' was released on April 12 1983, enough attention had already been focused on them to guarantee a fair hearing. Their first line of attack, the increasingly important proliferation of college radio stations, immediately fell into line, propelling the record to the top of their airplay charts by the dozens and boosting the band's core following of students ten-fold.

The all-important taste makers among the press were equally excited, paving the band's tour across America with a red carpet of glowing reviews. *Rolling Stone* gave 'Murmur' an uncommonly high four stars ('intelligent, enigmatic, deeply involving'... it reveals a depth and cohesiveness to R.E.M.'); *Musician* ('R.E.M. has the most hypnotizing sound of any group playing rock today'), *Record* ('music of movement and portent, driven with vague obsession') and the *New York Times* ('... will sound as fresh ten years from now as it does today') all followed suit.

When these factors combined with a now sizeable grass roots following – growing daily thanks to a month-long tour

with The English Beat – the result was sales beyond both band and record label's wildest dreams. 'Murmur' showed up on the May 14 *Billboard* chart at 190, was top 100 a fortnight later and top 50 six weeks after that. At the beginning of August, with the revamped recording of 'Radio Free Europe' at number 78 in the singles charts (though they little knew it, the closest they would get to a hit for over four years), 'Murmur' reached a chart peak of number 26. It was a phenomenal start.

Why such relatively instant success? Much of it was to do with being in the right place at the right time. The American music industry found itself in an all-time trough at the beginning of the 1980s: disco had died overnight, southern rock was mortally wounded, and punk had not successfully translated from working class Britain to suburban America. Punk's meltdown movement, however, the amorphous 'new wave', looked like it could. America duly reached out to Britain's pop explosion of the early eighties like a drowning man to a liferaft. By the time 'Murmur' was released, the American chart was aflow with the likes of Soft Cell, Duran Duran, Culture Club, Haircut 100 and ABC: the fabled Second British Invasion.

R.E.M. benefited at both ends of this pendulum swing. Firstly, the American industry was obliged to unearth indigenous bands as well as accepting those handed them on a plate by the UK. Yet the majority of left-field American music – from The Dream Syndicate to Hüsker Dü – was too threatening for mainstream ears. Only R.E.M.'s wistful, subtle pop was pleasant enough to be played alongside the proliferation of pretty-boy English music while simultaneously making radio look adventurous.

In reviewing 'Radio Free Europe' in July '83 *Billboard*, the American industry Bible, admitted as much: "Even a few months ago, the dense, bass-heavy, thumping sound of

■ (Ed Colver)

this Athens, Georgia quartet would have been considered too abrasive for pop radio; but the airwaves are gradually opening up to what used to be underground music . . ."

R.E.M. too acknowledge that the winds of change were blowing in their favour. Talking to Britain's *Jamming!* magazine at the end of that year, Peter Buck explained how because of dwindling listening figures, radio had been "going through a real panic situation because they don't know what to play. Then they've been hiring all these guys – who also don't know what they're doing – to tell them what to do, and they say 'Play new music.' So what's new music? They don't know! We sneaked in the back door – 'Oh, they've got guitars, they're a little different, let's put them on . . .! We got a foot in the door through all the confusion."

While on the one hand riding high on the crest of the 'British Invasion' as America's possible counterparts, R.E.M.'s own disdain for such vacuous pop and loyalty to the old-fashioned virtues of a long, sweaty live show reinforced their status among the real new music fans, the ones who went out to clubs every night of the week. R.E.M. were at the commercial end of America's new underground, but as card-carrying members they received unflagging support from those fans.

Packaging also once again played its part in selling something more than a sixties garage group with art-folk pretensions. For a record brimming over with southern exoticism, dressing the sleeve up in kudzu, the all-pervasive creeping vine of Georgia, was an inspired touch. Yet 'Murmur's' meticulous attention to detail, believe those close to its creation, was often misinterpreted as one glorious error.

"The sophisticated aspects of the record were not appreci-ated right off the bat," says Don Dixon. "It was viewed as this naïve accidental thing, because nobody really knew who Mitch and I were in the industry. So since they didn't know us and we were southern, obviously we were really stupid, and we just stumbled across this stuff. And we were so dumb we didn't know how to make it into a real big record."

"It sounds like someone who's never mixed a record mixed the record," admits Peter Buck, but stresses that "We worked with two real pro mixers, we knew what we were doing . . . We didn't just find this thing. We had the songs written, we had them arranged, we knew what we were

■ **Washington D.C., March 1983.** (Laura Levine)

doing with the overdubs, we fought over mixes, we remixed stuff, we worked really hard to get it just like that. That was the record we wanted to make, and people tended to, at least in those days, just go 'Oh well, that must have been an accident.' No it wasn't. Mitch and Don went out on a limb to make a strange-sounding record."

Its strangest facet of all was, no doubt, its hide-and-seek vocals. The beauty of their tone aside, it was hard to decide which presented a greater challenge: interpreting the words where they were audible, or deciphering them where they weren't.

Over a period of time, the group were willing to give clues. 'Moral Kiosk' was "more or less a reaction to all those Jerry

Falwell-ish TV ministries", and 'Talk About The Passion' was saying "that passion is just something you experience, not talk about". 'We Walk' Michael admitted was an example of simply repeating other people's phrases, as naïve a lyric as its tune was childlike, yet 'Laughing' drew on Laöcoon, a freak mythological figure, for inspiration. '9-9' meanwhile, had an element of the wind-up about it. "It was purposely recorded," said Stipe, "so you could never be able to decipher any of the words except the very last phrase, which was 'conversation fear', which is what the song was about."

Occasionally the group's own interpretations differed, as with 'Perfect Circle'. Peter Buck recalled how in October '82, his emotions frayed through constant touring and lack of sleep, "I was standing in the City Gardens in Trenton, New Jersey at the back door and it was just getting dark. These kids were playing touch football, the last game before dark came, and for some reason I was so moved I cried for twenty minutes . . . I told Michael to try and capture that feeling. There's no football in there, no kids, no twilight. But it's all there."

Michael Stipe countered by saying "That song concerns my old girlfriend, and it was an intensely personal song to me. I really like that it can mean two different things. But the feeling is exactly the same as what I think about the song and what Peter thinks about the song. It's the exact same feeling but the details are different."

In the midst of such confusion, R.E.M.'s following worked with what they thought they could hear. During one interview, Stipe admitted that "There's a line in 'Sitting Still' that apparently sounds like 'We could gather, throw up beer'. And what it really says is 'We could gather, throw a fit'." To which a nearby fan exclaimed "You're kidding! I thought it said 'We could gather through our fear'."

"No, but that sounds great," replied Stipe. "I might use that. It's probably far superior to what I wrote, actually."

■　　■　　■

The music industry repeatedly held out its arms to R.E.M. in 1983, enticing them into its protective clutch with promises of fame and fortune. The group tentatively stepped forward, found themselves crushed by the giant's bearhug, and recoiled.

The first attempt at abduction was with the video for 'Radio Free Europe'. Michael Stipe proposed as a location the rural Paradise Gardens of Rev. Harold Finster to which the artist Scott Belville had pointed him. There was no connection with the song, but the words themselves were so indirect that a non-linear video almost made sense. They were thus filmed wandering aimlessly around the Gardens for hours on end.

I.R.S. were disappointed. Video was still a new medium, but the British pop bands who were dominating, and being broken by, the new cable television station MTV, all favored fast moving, colorful storylines. I.R.S. added footage of R.E.M. playing live, much to the group's chagrin. The group were even more dismayed that the final cost of the exercise was around half the $28,000 spent recording the album. "You hire two people to make the record, and eight people to make the video," notes Peter Buck. "I've never understood that." He had nothing but disdain for the medium. Michael Stipe merely longed for the opportunity to take full control of it.

Then on October 6, R.E.M. made their first major live television appearance, on 'Late Night with David Letterman'. The producers asked that the group's leader come up to the host's desk for an interview. R.E.M., having no leader, instead suggested Letterman come down to their level to talk. They won, the nervous host chatting briefly with Buck and Mills on the stage in between a rendition of 'Radio Free Europe' and an as-yet untitled new song (to become 'So. Central Rain'). Television working on the principle of stars

among stars, the garrulous Peter Buck was nonetheless paid twice that of the other members.

But the group's biggest dispute with the industry was over their greatest opportunity yet, opening for the now multi-platinum Police on the east coast. They had spent much of the past year on the road supporting The Gang of Four and The (English) Beat, groups they shared an affinity and an audience with, and were at last enjoying the prestige of selling out clubs as headliners. Opening for The Police in major Coliseums went beyond what they felt was the call of duty.

"We weren't ready to play 45 minutes in a place that big," says Buck. "We didn't have the right equipment, didn't have a sound man really, didn't have a light man. Then we were going to play to people who'd never heard of us, never gave a shit."

Ian Copeland had already found in failing to convince them to tour with the B-52's and The Clash that he himself had put forward the reasons for the group – or at least Bill Berry and Mike Mills – to say no.

"These guys had been listening to all my punk dogma. Part of what I was preaching all along, was how a band should play to ten people that came to see them, rather than playing to 1000 people who came to see someone else. And every single date The Police did in America, they never supported anyone. But that was mainly because there was no one to support. Well, R.E.M. remembered that and suddenly I was offering them all these tours and they were saying 'Nah, we'd rather do a club tour'. And I'd say 'But you're going to play to all these people', and they'd say 'Well Ian, don't you remember when you said . . .' It was funny. I'd say 'Guys, forget what I said!'"

In this particular case they finally acquiesced, agreeing to open for The Police over five shows at three indoor arenas, then at Shea Stadium in New York on August 18 and JFK Stadium in Philadelphia two days later. The money – $10,000 for 20 minutes at each of the outdoor shows – was no doubt a convincing factor.

In subsequent interviews over the years, R.E.M. gained great kudos from their pronounced distaste for the events, once calling them "the most wretched, abysmal experience of our lives". It's a viewpoint they still cling to.

"We knew it was gonna be horrible, but we got talked into

■ **Supporting The Police at Shea Stadium, August 18 1983. "A waste of fucking time," insists Peter Buck.** (Ebet Roberts)

it," says Buck. "It just taught us that we're pretty much right on these things. Everyone said that 'Oh, this will make you have a hit record', but we did the seven dates and we didn't sell one record out of that. It was a waste of fucking time."

"Very much a self-fulfilling prophecy," argues Jay Boberg on that point. "I'm not trying to say that those audiences were great, but R.E.M. could have blown them away, and I think they probably did. Those shows were probably a lot more successful in their career than they will ever acknowledge. But they hated the experience."

"I would guess they were probably miserable," says Ian Copeland. "First of all because of the fear of it all, plus they were the third act on [at the stadiums, they appeared before Joan Jett]. And they went out (at Shea) and played in the rain and probably thought they were terrible. But they didn't hear what I heard, from out in the audience. When they played 'Radio Free Europe' the whole crown went

fucking berserk. I looked up on the stage and there was these two kids I used to hang out with. My heart was going crazy. That was the moment I finally realised 'Shit! This isn't just my buddies out there. This band is going to make me rich! And I'm going to make them rich!' "

"I don't think anyone liked us," contests Buck. "I really don't think anyone did. I'm glad I got to play Shea Stadium, it was was cool. But the other dates were just boring."

Arguably, Buck was right in saying that The Police shows didn't sell R.E.M. records: 'Murmur' began a rapid downward chart slide that very week. But above the stairs at the R.E.M. offices in Athens, the last photo one sees before departing is taken from Shea Stadium's stage, the backs of R.E.M. silhouetted against a never-ending sea of umbrellas. Its central placement in their headquarters possibly says something about its central placement in their hearts.

■　■　■

■ **At a photo session to publicise 'Murmur', the group look distinctly uncomfortable toying with teenybop imagery.** (Laura Levine)

British rock 'n' roll fans were not proud that their country was dominating the American charts in 1983; they were actually deeply ashamed that the 'Second British Invasion' should be so shallow compared to that which conquered the States in the mid sixties and changed rock music's complexion for evermore. But, they insisted, America could only blame itself. It was apparent to even the most enlightened British musicologist that the rock scene there had dried up after London wrestled the capital of punk away from New York. America's idea of 'new wave' had proved laughable, The Cars and The Knack with their skinny ties and insipid songs, and the hard core scene was obviously leading up a blind alley. There seemed to be no American band of worth walking a middle path.

Launched into this environment at the end of August, boosted by its American success, 'Murmur' was an instant critics' delight. The three major music papers, *NME*, *Melody Maker* and *Sounds* were all hustled into running stories on R.E.M. by their American correspondents, eager to spread the word. The readers of these papers, used to being bombarded with critical hype, prepared to be disappointed.

But I.R.S. Records, strong in Britain ever since Miles Copeland had built his business there, were determined to prove otherwise, and when the influential Friday night television programme *The Tube* offered R.E.M. a chance to play live on the show, I.R.S. willingly fronted the money to bring the band over, arranging live dates at London's Dingwalls on November 19, The Marquee three days later and a visit to France after that. Appearing on *The Tube* on November 18, R.E.M. introduced themselves to British audiences by performing 'Radio Free Europe', 'So. Central Rain' and 'Talk About The Passion' with typical élan. The two London shows were packed to the rafters.

The memory of that night at The Marquee remains vividly etched on the author's memory. Compared to the perfection of image that typified Britain's new pop culture, R.E.M. plumbed the depths of fashion, Michael Stipe wearing an ugly sweater in a club where temperatures frequently hit the 100° mark and Mike Mills looking, as ever, like the all-American high-school graduate. While Bill Berry pounded out the beat at the back, Peter Buck, shirt flapping wildly, chased his Rickenbacker around the stage with the same enthusiasm as Pete Townshend in the days of 'The Who before they signed a record contract' at the same club almost twenty years before.

■ Michael Stipe as Bob Dylan during filming of Laura Levine's 'Just Like A Movie', a low budget super-8 parody of a Dylan-Donovan film. Featuring many of Athens' musical luminaries, it has never been publicly shown. (Laura Levine)

English audiences used to a comfortable 45-minute set even from headliners at major concerts were amazed when R.E.M. almost doubled that in the heated club. Stipe, who had started off motionless, clinging protectively to his microphone, ended the show tumbling all over the stage with the same disregard for personal safety as Buck. When they finally left the stage, The Marquee's walls were soaking wet.

Walking back out into the Soho night air, wrote a reviewer in the *NME*, 'I found myself dazed and reborn. This is the most vital American group of today.'

R.E.M. weren't so sure. "We like to think of ourselves as the tip of the iceberg," said Peter Buck to *Jamming!* magazine. "We're not the most commercial band in the world, but we're one of the more accessible of the new American bands. It's one of our duties while we're over here to say 'It's not a wasteland over there'. There are great bands in the mid-west that you'll never hear unless you go to their town."

That was liable to change.

■ ■ ■

Every group relishes good press, and R.E.M. are no exception. But even the four young men whose moderate success thus far owed a lot to the hyperbole of America's print taste makers must have felt overwhelmed – and not a little overburdened – when the various critics' polls for the year 1983 hit the news stands.

The writers at *Rolling Stone* named 'Murmur' their Album of the Year above Michael Jackson's 'Thriller', The Police's 'Synchronicity' and U2's 'War'. These same critics also rated R.E.M. Best New Artist and even third Top Band. The *Village Voice*, whose Pazz and Jop Poll is perhaps America's most prestigious, were almost as generous, placing 'Murmur' second only to 'Thriller' in the year's best albums, while *Record*, *Trouser Press* and the *LA Times* all pitched in with similarly high ratings.

Such bestowals of praise – saying much more for 'Murmur's' lasting influence than its modest sales of around 170,000 – could easily have rendered the group uncomfortable in recording its follow-up. But by the time these unanimous jury verdicts were announced, America's great white hope already had their second album in the can and were keeping busy by playing cover songs in local bars.

Aware that their two I.R.S. releases to date had presented the moody, restrained side of the band, R.E.M. determined that their second album should be harder-edged and more song-orientated, a closer approximation of their live set. As a result of the continual live work and the confidence that went with their growing status, they were writing new material at a rate they would never equal, and a week before going to Europe, they put down a staggering 22 songs in one day in San Francisco with Elliot Mazer, Neil Young's producer.

Although Mazer's name was briefly mooted as a possible

(Tom Sheehan)

album producer, there was never much doubt that the group would return to the partnership and environment that had served them so well on their first vinyl outing. Over two stretches of eight consecutive days either side of Christmas, they recorded 'Reckoning' – a title acknowledging and, by its very context, digging at the seriousness with which a second album is viewed – with almost effortless ease.

"They were on a roll," recalls Mitch Easter, who says he felt an unspoken understanding to ignore 'Murmur's' surprise success, rather than get bogged down trying to emulate it. "We knew that was the worst thing we could do. The minute you start to get into deliberate music you screw up, I think. And the thing that they had that was so attractive was this sort of ease of writing these nice songs. We didn't want to lose that by over-analyzing them."

These songs were a disparate collection, reflecting the group's refusal to pigeon-hole themselves, and Easter recognised the problems of collating such varied material on to one record. "When I heard the songs they had, I kept saying at the time – tongue in cheek, but not totally – that this record would be like their Led Zeppelin II, (which) was supposedly made in different studios all over the place because they were touring. R.E.M. were in the same position in a way: they'd had some success with the first record, they were on their way up, and they weren't making as much of a unified record. But maybe those songs would express that band-on-the-move feel. That live sound always appealed to them back in those days, and so I thought, maybe we can get that on this record."

They did, largely by refusing to labor over the process, as Mike Mills made clear a few months later in describing the group's recording techniques. "We go in there and we just knock out the basic tracks on first or second take. The

vocals are pretty much the same way. We even use the reference vocals sometimes, because the more you do it, the less spontaneous it becomes. It sounds like you're trying real hard to get it perfect. But if you just go ahead and knock out the tracks and vocals, you can spend most of your time getting whatever overdubs you want and doing the mixdown. That's where we spent ten out of our fourteen days in the studio, remixing."

The speed of recording was of great pride to R.E.M. On the sleeve to 'Reckoning' they listed fourteen day's work, and Peter Buck quickly chopped three of those off in interviews. To Dixon and Easter, this seemed like so much good copy.

"We were here at least 25 days," insists Dixon. "And I was here eighteen hours a day every day of that period."

"When I read 'eleven days', I thought, 'What the fuck!'" agrees Easter. "It was twenty days, which was still short, but it's not eleven."

But the Reflection diaries list only sixteen days, and confirm the group's proud claim that they even cancelled studio time, much to I.R.S.'s amazement. And, points out Peter Buck, "We took a day off to play at Friday's (the pizza restaurant in Greensboro, which was closing), and we took a night off to see a movie. We took a day off to shoot the video too, in the studio." He does, however, allow for the intensity of recording. "We would work until three or four in

the morning, then Don and Mitch would get there at 10.00 ... So by midnight those guys would be exhausted."

Don Dixon, who recalls "just being completely burned out" at the end of recording, nonetheless stresses his enthusiasm for the speedy process. "We were making the records very quickly by the period's standards. You can make records that are better thematically by making them quicker, where you don't have the luxury of second-guessing yourself."

The result with 'Reckoning' was a roughly-hewn celebration of spontaneity, yet one embodied by a clarity of production and maturity of songwriting that would once more outshine its contemporaries.

At its rawest extreme was 'Pretty Persuasion', which has come to represent the 'archetypal' R.E.M. anthem, a simplistic lead guitar motif paving the way for a verse built on emotive if inscrutable choral harmonies, underlined by ringing guitars and thrusting drums; as with most R.E.M. songs, rather than the series of catchphrases that become a traditional chorus, the focus is on a concise, repetitive refrain. And at all times, the song bristles with a wanton energy.

'Pretty Persuasion' had been in the set since 1981, when, according to Peter, "Michael had a dream three nights in a row that he was a photographer taking the last Rolling Stones picture sleeve. They were all sitting in a dock with their feet in the water and the cover was 'Pretty Persuasion'."

A Rolling Stones reference could also apply to the equally abrasive 'Second Guessing', the arrogant challenge "Why are you trying to second guess me . . . Who will be your book this season?" met with the joyous refrain of "Here we are" that many saw as reminiscent of an equally young and confident Jagger and Co.

But 'Reckoning's' central theme was not so much the bravado apparent on the record's louder cuts as the watery metaphors elsewhere, beginning with the working title printed on the spine, 'File Under Water' (which also doubled as a joke at the group's lack of easy categorisation), and evolving over the three opening songs.

'Harborcoat', the first of these, is one of the least fathomable of all R.E.M. numbers, Stipe's own band mates admitting little comprehension. Likewise, 'Seven Chinese Brothers' appears at first to be little more than a play on the

proverb of the five Chinese brothers, one of whom could hold the ocean in his mouth, and 'So. Central Rain (I'm Sorry)' is ostensibly a straight narrative about severe flooding in Athens, with the phone lines down and R.E.M. unable to contact their hometown from on tour. But these two songs, along with 'Camera', are also a hymn to a departed friend: Carol Levy died in a car accident in the spring of '83, as did two passengers. Her memory lived on in the promise "She will return" from 'Seven Chinese Brothers', the helpless cry "I'm Sorry" from 'So. Central Rain', and the forlorn question "Will she be remembered?" from 'Camera'.

This exorcism of emotions helped R.E.M. conjure up some of their most inspired music. 'Time After Time' emulated the haunted spirit of the most possessed of Velvet Underground songs, while 'Camera' was an equally moving, if more traditionally-structured ballad, replete with ghostly effects and a gentle guitar solo. On 'So. Central Rain', the sense of grief even overcame Michael Stipe. As he emitted a hollow, wordless cry at the song's finale, he fell off balance and down the stairs that he sang from, breaking a microphone

■ (Ed Colver)

in the process; hence his voice's sudden fade before the end of the song.

The theme of departure was further continued with '(Don't Go Back To) Rockville', reluctantly recorded in one take to humor its number one fan, Bertis Downs and, as a joke, slowed down from its original thrash into a gentle country song in the process. The result was almost unearthly beautiful, its emotive performance carrying an appeal that crossed musical continents. It became a standard of the new American underground, and a monument to Mike Mills' songwriting ability.

'Reckoning's' finale was 'Little America', a "perverse view of us driving around the country seeing things that are really nice and really horrible," said Peter Buck. Michael Stipe seemed unsure which was which. "Another Greenville, another Magic Mart," he shouted at the generic mid-America R.E.M. had just spent three years driving through, before delivering an in-joke jibe at their manager and hapless navigator, "Jefferson, I think we're lost". R.E.M. were anything but lost and they knew it. They were merely exploring a possible vocation as storytellers of small time America.

On an album submerged in mournful lyrics, 'Little America' was almost the only occasion when R.E.M.'s humor and playfulness surfaced. Their lighter side was mostly saved for the plethora of B-sides and out-takes, such as when Michael Stipe – who at one point in the sessions emerged from his stairwell to announce he had been singing naked – proved reluctant to lend 'Seven Chinese Brothers' the energy his producers wanted. Don Dixon found an old gospel album and threw it to Stipe who, enthralled by the liner notes, was recorded singing them. That became 'Voice Of Harold'; 'Seven Chinese Brothers' was taped, with the emotion Dixon had sought, immediately afterwards.

There was also a night of live recordings as had worked so well during 'Murmur'. "We took a little while off so everybody could come back in and be in the mood to do it like a show," recalls Mitch Easter. The group seized on the opportunity to get uproariously drunk, recording only a proposed commercial for Walter's Bar-B-Q in Athens, and a tuneless rendition of 'King Of The Road.' At other points during the session, however, they recorded 'Ages Of You' again – as fine a song as they would ever discard – 'Burning Down', a heavy metal stomp 'Burning Hell', two

■ At Walter's Bar-B-Q, a favorite eating place at Athens. R.E.M. recorded a mock advertisement for Walter's during the 'Reckoning' sessions which ended up on various B-sides and 'Dead Letter Office'. (Laura Levine)

■ **Among Bill Miller's whirlygigs, Gainesville, Georgia, filming 'Left Of Reckoning'.** (Laura Levine)

versions of 'Windout' (the better one with Jefferson singing), 'Mystery To Me', 'Just A Touch', and acoustic versions of 'Gardening At Night' and the Velvets' 'Pale Blue Eyes' and 'Femme Fatale'. I.R.S. would get not just their B-sides but half a future album from these supposedly superfluous ideas.

Determined to have more control over a video, R.E.M. brought in Atlanta film-maker Howard Libov to shoot 'So. Central Rain' in the studio at Reflection, succumbing to the pressure of being seen performing only to the extent of playing behind screens. The compromise worked for both industry and band: although the group were evidently there in front of the camera, they were still playing hide and seek with the public. Michael Stipe, refusing to lip synch, made the unusual step of singing live to tape.

Stipe was keen to experiment further with the video medium and secured the backing for an art piece that would accompany the entire first side of 'Reckoning'. His idea, similar to that of the 'Radio Free Europe' video, was to spend a day at primitive sculptor Bill Miller's whirligig gardens in Gainesville, Georgia. He recruited the Athens painter and film maker Jim Herbert to make it.

"The idea was that I would be more sympathetic, and the band respected me as an artist," says Herbert, who saw a connection between Stipe's lyrical approach and the choice of location. "A lot of his lyrics seem to be built on collecting art phrases and just putting them together, and there's a kind of letting things happen, letting things fall into place, that some of the primitives have."

As a result, Herbert produced something as equally unspecific as the group's music. After shooting them walking and running among the whirligigs, he then used the 'rephotography' method to edit, a process that involves taking photographs of finished frames at random, closing in or pulling back from them with no preconception of what is coming next. "It's really a new film occasion," he explains. "With 'Reckoning', there was no attempt to edit the music, and as it happens, the way the songs came up on the album, and the images that were done, were uncannily related . . . I think the band understands that layered process, especially back with their early music where things were so layered and diffused. Michael knows about muddling through – he knows about the grey areas out of which clarity comes."

'Left Of Reckoning', as the project was called, had limited outlets, but I.R.S. did use Herbert's film for the promotion of 'Pretty Persuasion'. "It was a very unorthodox video for that time," says Herbert. "But it just seemed like within weeks that there were lots of those kind of videos out."

Michael Stipe also took control of the album sleeve, bringing a drawing of a two-headed snake to Howard Finster and suggesting he turn it into a fully-fledged painting. Stipe later described it as an attempt to define the elements: "Part of it is rocks and part of it is the sun and part of it the sky." However, his attempts at a long-distance painting partnership – let alone the problems of reproducing a Finster artwork on an album sleeve – led to disappointment with the final product.

There were people at A&M, I.R.S.'s parent company, who were dismayed that their supposed group-most-likely-to were even *thinking* of releasing a record in such a dishevelled sleeve. But the purposely-askew snapshots on the back and the handwritten notes on the inside, particularly coming after the cultured finesse of 'Murmur', suggest that 'Reckoning' was a deliberate step back into the garage, and that R.E.M. had decided they did not yet wish to meet the masses head on.

■ ■ ■

Having been on the road almost continually since first discovering the joys of that lifestyle back in July 1980, R.E.M. used a long-overdue break between finishing 'Reckoning' in January 1984 and getting back on tour to promote its release in April, to reacquaint themselves with their hometown.

Athens had changed considerably over just five years, from a conservative college town with a fringe artistic community into one of the most envied musical hotspots in the country. The varying success of the B-52's, Pylon and now R.E.M. – along with R.E.M.'s proclamation in interviews that the University of Georgia "is known all through the south as a place where if you couldn't hack it anywhere else you'd go there and fuck and drink your way through school" – proved an irresistible magnet for the region's would-be bohemians. Students moved to Athens and formed bands not because there was nothing else to do, as R.E.M.'s generation insisted was the case, but because it seemed the right thing to do, thus helping the town to enter a continual self-perpetuating period of activity – and to lose its innocence.

The club scene – which had received a serious setback in 1982 when Tyrone's burnt down with no insurance policy – grew as an increasingly larger potential live audience made itself visible. The 40 Watt Club expanded from its College Avenue loft to the site of the old Koffee Klub on Clayton Street and then up to Broad Street, where it flourished as the hub of activity for local music. The spacious Uptown Lounge, formerly just a drinking bar, then also started booking local and touring bands in late 1983.

R.E.M. themselves had long outgrown these venues, playing the 1000 capacity I&I Club as early as 1981, and the University's free outdoor shows at Legion Field in June '82 and October '83. By March '84, when they played two nights at the 1200-capacity Madhatter, they recognised the danger of becoming godlike in their home town, and opted to make Atlanta the official home show on future national tours.

But Athens was still their residence and nothing was going to change that. The myth that groups had to move to the music biz capitals of New York and Los Angeles to make it was proving only slightly less transparent than the one dictating that all good management should also be based there. Jefferson Holt, finding that he could far better represent his clients' desires by being close to them than by being close to the industry, had rented a small office on College Square, employed Sandi Phipps as secretary the same month he split with her as lover, and continued to handle the group with the same laid-back confidence he had always displayed.

Surrounded by creativity, R.E.M. could not stop working in the new year of 1984 just because the calendar had some empty spaces in it. While Michael Stipe immersed himself in the visual presentation of the group, his three partners decided to return to being a sloppy bar band playing silly pop songs.

The notion of an alter-ego was not unfamiliar to them, having spent Halloween '83, with Michael, opening for The Cramps at New York's Peppermint Lounge as the suitably horrific It Crawled From The South; now they decided to become The Hindu Love Gods, a long-cherished would-be band name of Peter's, and asked Bryan Cook, who had been establishing an extrovert's reputation of his own with his band Is Ought Gap, to sing.

■ **The Hindu Love Gods: Mike Mills, Warren Zevon, Bill Berry, Bryan Cook and Peter Buck.** (Sandra-Lee Phipps)

Cook joined the others in Bill Berry's front room, singing through a practice amp, working up a set close to that with which R.E.M. had first started out with, "songs that Michael was tired of doing and wouldn't sing anymore, or that somebody else was tired of doing," as Cook puts it. These included 'Permanent Vacation' and 'Narrator', "All these songs that I remembered from three years before, that were just killer ... And I got to sing them!"

The Hindu Love Gods made their live debut at the 40 Watt Club in January 1984, hiring a limousine to drive them all of three blocks to the club and play up their supposed stardom. Nobody turned up early enough to get the joke. The 40 Watt was nonetheless packed by the time they took the stage that night, as was Bourbon Street, a former strip bar in the basement of the Georgia Hotel, when The Hindu Love Gods performed with new bands Kilkenny Cats and Dreams So Real.

The three playing members of R.E.M. also kept busy recording demos with 'Werewolves Of London' legend Warren Zevon, who was searching for a new record deal after years out of the music scene. R.E.M. invited him to Athens to record at John Keane's studio there in the spring, and enjoyed the learning process of being someone else's session band. And when they found themselves with a couple of free hours, the opportunity to record a Hindu Love Gods single seemed too good to miss.

The live versions recorded that day of 'Narrator' and 'The Easybeats' 'Gonna Have A Good Time Tonight', with Bryan Cook singing and Warren Zevon on piano, were typically exuberant, and would eventually see the light of day on I.R.S. in 1986. The five-piece even made a brief Love Gods appearance that same week at the 40 Watt as part of the encores of Love Tractor's own covers band, Wheel O'Cheese.

The Hindu Love Gods lived on in spirit – years later, when glam rock songwriter and producer Mike Chapman heard that his 'Little Willy' and 'Tiger Feet' were part of the makeshift group's live set, he volunteered his production services to Peter Buck – but spirit alone.

■ ■ ■

Unlike 'Murmer', 'Reckoning' was not an obvious classic album. Whereas the group's debut presented an unusual and carefully crafted sound that carried twelve extraordinary songs along in its wake, the follow-up was a less cohesive collection of material rejoicing in variety and spontaneity. As Mitch Easter puts it, "'Murmur' is this thing called 'Murmur' whereas 'Reckoning' is just album number two."

But in presenting such an honest self-portrait, R.E.M. showed themselves to be a rock 'n' roll group in every sense of the word, a decisive move. For however successfully musicians can come together in the studio incognisant of each other and produce excellent – or at least popular – results, it is the groups that go down in history.

And as much as it may be about bringing together a number of talented musicians, a group is essentially a boys' club for eternal adolescents whose collective adventures become an ongoing public saga. The Beatles were the first and most successful group to sell the world this notion of eternal friendships, the public falling for the four Liverpool lads' camaraderie as much as for their music until ultimately the two became inseparable.

From then on, the myth of the great band as an impenetrable gang has proven impossible to shake. It mattered not that members of The Who were known to punch each other out on and off stage but that they did it out of love. And as The Rolling Stones' partnership of Mick Jagger and Keith Richards grew farther away from each other during the 1980's, the issue at stake with their fans became not whether they should divorce, but that as a 'married' couple, one should expect both highs and lows.

In 1984 it became apparent that R.E.M. had a similarly indefinable chemistry. They were four very disparate identities who came together with perfect symmetry; each had individual qualities a fan could relate to, yet they performed together with the spirit of one. They were the gang that everyone wanted to be part of.

There was Michael Stipe, the artist. A lyricist who gave little of himself away, sang in riddles and metaphors and was at his most content working with visual imagery; whose love of his partners was total, but who preferred isolation.

There was Peter Buck, the rocker. A music fan of unusual sincerity who longed for nothing more than the next opportunity to get on stage and play; whose reputation for partying preceded him and whose opinions he could not keep to himself.

There was Mike Mills, the musician. A classically-trained performer accomplished on several instruments and responsible for the intriguing nuances that so distinguished his group's music; whose studied expression belied his sense of adventure.

There was Bill Berry, the businessman. An intelligent, hard-working professional who put paid to the myth that drummers were followers, not leaders; whose determination saw the group through many an early obstacle and whose songwriting contribution was not to be ignored.

R.E.M. were not unique in having these virtues. But they were certainly the first potentially successful American group to emerge for a long time in which such wide-ranging ingredients produced such an intoxicating single-minded whole.

All this was obvious to the press, who almost fell over each other in the rush to say so in the loudest tones possible. 'How much better can they possibly get?' asked *Musician*; 'There is no richer pop music being made today', opined *Record*; 'These guys seem to know exactly where they're going', observed *Rolling Stone*. In Britain, where reviews are rarely pedestrian, the *NME*'s Mat Snow successfully wrote himself into R.E.M. history with his talk of 'vinyl cathedrals' from 'one of the most beautifully exciting groups on the planet', and his belief that 'When I get to heaven, the angels will be playing not harps but Rickenbackers. And they will playing songs by R.E.M. . .'

Record buyers promptly propelled 'Reckoning' into the Billboard Top 30 only a month after its April 16 release, keeping it at No. 27 throughout June, and in the 200 for almost a full year (even if 'So. Central Rain' made but a small dent on the Hot 100 and 'Rockville' not even that).

While it would have been very easy for the group to ride in to mass acceptance on this wave of adulation and leave their contenders behind, R.E.M. had no intentions of severing any ties with their peer group. As they came to grasp the extent of their possible influence in America, the confidence that had always accompanied them turned into a defiant arrogance, the manner of which had rarely been seen among American bands on the verge of 'making it'.

R.E.M.'s knowledge of the media's workings had been apparent to its fellow students from the start. Peter Buck and Michael Stipe did not spend years reading the rock press during their teens not to learn the importance of image and how to deliver good copy. Therefore, their early interviews were festooned with embellishments and white lies. Indeed, Peter's willingness not to let facts get in the way of a good story had long ago led friends to place such anecdotes in 'Buckland', wherein an audience of 50 became 6, one of 300 became 800, 14 days turned into 11, and an angry reaction by a crowd of soldiers was a near escape with one's life.

There was nothing particularly dishonest or even original about this approach; in fact, R.E.M. seemed to adopt it almost out of respect to the tradition of rock 'n' roll. But there was certainly planning behind it. It only escaped into the press once that Mike Mills had been arrested for "cavorting nude with a young lady on a water tower"; like Buck's early assertion that "We're not much of a drinking band", it was important they did not appear as decadent as the pre-punk dinosaurs. That honesty was not always encouraged was proven when Jefferson publicly admonished Peter Buck for admitting in an early *Rolling Stone* article to earning only $350 a month. "Some day," said Holt, "You guys just might be making money, and then some reporter can say. 'Well Mr bigshott rock star, how much are you making now?' " Buck admitted to earning $24,000 before songwriting royalties in 1985, after which, as their income spiralled, such honesty duly clammed up.

Sometimes the quotes were so perverse that it was hard to believe journalists were not merely playing along, as when the group collectively denied an affinity with The Byrds while at the same time introducing the band's 'So You Wanna Be A Rock 'n' Roll Star' into their set, or when they gained credibility for turning down support tours with The Clash and The Go-Go's while supporting anyone from Bow Wow Wow through to Squeeze, The (English) Beat and The Police.

Yet there was a genuine integrity beneath many of their fibs. R.E.M. honestly did prefer headlining the small clubs to opening at the big stadiums, they really did record chart albums faster than anyone else of their stature, and they truly did disdain the old-fashioned glory of rock 'n' roll. Michael Stipe's most common quote during 1983 – "On the ladder of important things in this world, being in a rock band is probably on a lower rung, but then again, being Secretary of State is probably way down there too," – was well-rehearsed but it was sincere.

Throughout 1984, R.E.M. made it clear that if they were going to climb that ladder, they wanted to bring the new underground up with them. They took The Dream Syndicate and the dB's on tour with them. They enthused about harder-edged bands at every turn. Peter Buck not only played on the Replacements' album 'Let It Be' but reviewed it for a leading rock magazine. They toured Britain – twice – and not only chastised the pompous attitudes they encountered there, but included songs by The Replacements and Jason And The Scorchers in their set. And on the I. R. S. production 'The Cutting Edge', which was broadcast on MTV in July of that year, they went to town.

"Pop music for most people is really bland," said Peter Buck. "You don't have to understand it, it's just this boring little nothing. It's just cheeze whiz for the airwaves. That's

■ **During the recording for the I.R.S.-MTV production 'The Cutting Edge'.** (Ed Colver)

what people buy now: they don't buy something because it's exciting, they buy it because it's bland enough that they can put it on at home and it won't bother them. Most of the bands that I like are a little bit more threatening. R.E.M. is the wimpiest band that I like, and I'm not even sure that I like us yet."

"Me neither," said Mike Mills, who elaborated, "most of the people that we think are great you'll never hear about unless you're into music enough to go and find this stuff at local record stores. You won't find it at the big chains, and you'll never hear it on the radio. It's a real shame that radio is so locked into a format that very few good things ever get played."

"Fanzines are great, college radio is great," continued Buck. "Everything else about the music business just stinks at this point. And it's really a shame too, because I think right now America is having the best music ever. . . And I think it's your duty as Americans to go out and buy Black Flag. Buy our records: what the hell, it doesn't hurt me any!"

Looking back at this outspokenness, Buck comments that "I just didn't want to be one of those showbiz careerists: 'Oh yes, all the little people that made me the man that I am'. Fuck that. We were playing every city and there'd be great bands and no one would go see 'em, and then some guy with a funny haircut from a foreign country would come over with one record that was unplayably bad and get 800 people, and that was the hippest thing in the world. It was infuriating. We wanted to reiterate that we hadn't completely sprung out of nowhere. We came from a post-punk perspective where a lot of people were doing the same things, and maybe we were a little bit more commercial, but there was no difference between us and Pylon, or Black Flag."

In April '84, an angry Buck told the British weekly *Sounds* that at home, "American bands don't get signed, American bands don't get promoted, American bands don't get played on the radio. The only thing the industry is interested in is leasing the latest British album to get a piece of the supposed 'invasion' action. There's no money left for new American outfits."

In the October issue of American magazine *Record*, he put pen to paper in an essay entitled 'The True Spirit Of American Rock', inspired by "the complacency of the music business" in England where "shocked laughter greeted my assertions that there are plenty of good bands making exciting music in America."

By the end of the year, he had obviously seen an improvement, telling *Jamming!* that "Suddenly an audience has sprung up who don't listen to the British invasion bullshit and are slowly returning to American groups. Three years ago there wasn't anyone making interesting records in America, but in the last year a lot of bands have come up from nowhere."

R.E.M.'s attitude towards the British wasn't entirely fair on a country that was welcoming them, on a cult level at least, with open arms. A six date British tour in the spring and a 14-date excursion in the autumn – during which they played to 1500 people in London and performed live on another prestigious TV show, *The Whistle Test* – proved that there was an audience eager to hear new American music.

■ **Leeds, England, during the 1984 spring tour. At far right is Jefferson Holt.** (Cheshire)

But only those acts with the support of major labels could afford to follow them over. This included Jason And The Scorchers and Violent Femmes, but it didn't allow for Hüsker Dü or The Replacements. And although I. R. S. sank large sums of money into breaking R.E.M. in Britain, the chances of an all-important hit single there remained remote. On continental Europe, progress was even slower, the group's dates in Germany bombing so badly that other American bands had their tours cancelled as a direct consequence.

■ **Performing 'Do You Belive In Magic' at New Jersey's Capital Theatre for MTV's 'Rock Influences' show on 'Folk Rock' with the song's composer, Jon Sebastian.** (Sandra-Lee Phillips)

In America their standing grew ever greater. MTV selected them to exemplify the 'folk rock' segment of a series called 'Rock Influences'.

R.E.M.'s influences were a source of common discussion over these first couple of years in the public eye. The distinct jangle of Buck's Rickenbacker guitar was obviously reminiscent of The Byrds, and when MTV presented the chance, they were delighted to share the stage with former Byrd Roger McGuinn. Yet Peter Buck continued to insist that the influence was second generation, that he was greater inspired by Big Star or the Soft Boys, a much-maligned British neo-pyschedelic group who featured a similar style of playing. As if to prove the point, he and former Soft Boy Robyn Hitchcock, who was now recording and performing solo, began teaming up with alarming regularity.

Being likened to The Band was not such a problem. R.E.M. felt they could identify with the team camaraderie, easy-going vocal style and deep south pleasantries of the group Bob Dylan chose to tour and record with in the sixties and early seventies. Appearing on 'Rock Influences' with Rick Danko was another personal highlight for them.

When visiting Britain, R.E.M. were beseiged with infuriating comparisons to The Smiths, the country's finest new rock group in years. The Smiths walked a similarly tantalising path between being staunchly underground and massively successful. They too juggled a Rickenbacker jangle with an eccentric singer: Morrissey's avowed celibacy was as removed from the hardened partying of the other Smiths as Stipe's artistry was from the pure rock 'n' roll spirit of *his* bandfellows. It is likely that being perceived as a lesser Smiths in Britain – even though they had been making records some three years longer – contributed to R.E.M.'s dissatisfaction with the UK.

By the end of 1984, however, as dozens of new garage bands adopted 'Radio Free Europe' as their favourite cover version, it was R.E.M. who were considered influential. They performed over 100 shows in 1984 on three continents, recorded and played under pseudonyms, and guested on other people's records. R.E.M. were furthering their reputation as the hardest working new band in America. They had no reason to imagine that it wouldn't continue to be the most fun career in the world.

But it wouldn't.

■   ■   ■

O

On the return leg of a business swing through Europe
in the spring of 1985, Jay Boberg took the opportunity to
visit R.E.M. while they were mixing their new album in
London. He expected the familiarly happy scenario he had
always encountered at Reflection in North Carolina.
Instead, he walked in on an atmosphere that could be cut
with a knife.

"There were a lot of problems," he recounts. "There was a
real strain. It was the first time I was in the studio where I
didn't feel like everyone was having a good time."

Everyone wasn't having a good time. In fact, everyone was
having the most miserable time of their lives.

The problems had started with R.E.M.'s determination to
get straight back into the studio for a third album.
'Reckoning' had come together easily and besides, their
decision not to take large advances off I.R.S. meant that
they could not afford to stay off the road for too long. A
lucrative tour of colleges during the peak season of spring
parties necessitated that they finish the new album by then
or hold its release until the autumn. This would not have
been a disastrous option but, determined to set a furious
work rate and full of youthful zeal, they opted for the former
path.

Recognizing the many options in the recording world and
the limited time in which to try them all, they had already
decided to end the successful partnership with Mitch
Easter and Don Dixon. With Easter's group Let's Active now
full-time I.R.S. recording artistes, Dixon pursuing a solo
career, and the result of 'Murmur' and 'Reckoning' ensuring
that lucrative production opportunities awaited their every
spare day, the North Carolinians were not unduly perturbed.

But R.E.M. left the search for a replacement until the

last moment. Peter Buck suggested the English-based
American Joe Boyd, whose work with Fairport Convention,
Richard Thompson and Nick Drake made him an ideal
candidate with whom to further explore R.E.M.'s folk-rock
roots. Boyd, however, was booked. After a month during
which no better options came up, Joe Boyd called R.E.M.
from Canada, where the project he was meant to be working
on had just fallen through. Did R.E.M. still need a producer?
The answer being affirmative, Boyd jumped straight on a
plane to Atlanta, and after a day spent recording demos
with the band, was hired. Boyd suggested they work at his
preferred studio in London, and given that he now had time
on his hands, that they start immediately. Within ten days
of the two parties meeting, they were working together in
London.

Many a record company would have refused to endorse a
hefty album budget on the basis of such a brief encounter.
But I.R.S. were left with little choice, Holt keeping Jay
Boberg from interfering by telling him that R.E.M. were
going to London only to do demos. In the process, by
preventing the record company and producer from cement-
ing a relationship, R.E.M. put Boyd in an awkward position.
"The record company was working for them, and I was
working for them," Boyd says of the group's attitude, "and
that was a slightly unusual experience for me. That was
probably one of the most difficult things for me to adjust
to." He is unsure that he ever did.

Boyd had not been overly familiar with R.E.M.'s music
before the first enquiring phone call, only aware that
"Sometimes you hear about a record and you just know
from the kind of confidence with which it's released that
it's good." Buying the albums proved his instinct correct,
but also confirmed Easter and Dixon's worst suspicions by
giving them the impression that they were "a little raw and

■ (Peter Anderson)

unsophisticated from a sound point of view." Only when back in London awaiting the group did he realise that "Those two records were actually great, and the sound is perfectly suited to the band." At which "I got a bit more nervous about it, because I realised they wouldn't be quite so easy to improve upon."

The group were experiencing their own trepidation, discovering that they had a week and a half to write the best part of an album: of the songs that would finally make it on to the album only 'Old Man Kensey', 'Auctioneer' and 'Driver 8' had so far been exercised live.

One further element that neither group nor producer had fully taken into consideration was the change of environment. R.E.M. came from a hot, wet climate. London in March was cold and damp. And whereas in Charlotte they were used to being just minutes from the studio, Boyd's location was on the outskirts of London, entailing either a long, arduous journey through traffic if they decided to use the driver provided them, or an even more tiresome voyage by public transport if they came in on their own.

The result of all this was a lack of direction. "It's the only time we've walked in and didn't have a clue," says Buck. "We had this batch of songs that we'd written really fast, with not even the beginning of an idea on how to make them. We couldn't agree on tempos, we'd argue about things like keys. . . We forgot some of the things you have to remember, like you have to know what you're doing."

Homesick, fatigued and unsure of themselves, R.E.M. began to wonder if this was all worth it. As a group, they had achieved more than in their wildest dreams, playing every venue from biker bars to baseball stadiums, becoming cult stars and leaving a mark on 1980's American rock that would remain even were they to break up tomorrow. Now they were a business, signing pay cheques, employing staff, and under pressure to deliver 'crossover' records and 'commercial' videos. Even worse, there was no clear break visible in their schedule for the rest of the year. The idea of breaking up tomorrow suddenly became very appealing.

■ **The underground quickly took to R.E.M. in Britain, but mainline success proved harder to come by.** (Tom Sheehan)

"We were all looking at each other," recalls Buck, "going 'We're probably going back to the nicest weather in the nicest town to have spring in the entire world, and we're only going to be there for four days, and then we're going to be gone until Christmas.' We started thinking 'Maybe we should just cancel this and enjoy the springtime, and then who cares whether the record sells or not?' "

Jefferson Holt, aware that this year they could at last capitalize on the work of the five before, rallied them together: they could be a part-time band and sell maybe 100,000 albums a time *if* that's what they wanted, he told them, but wouldn't they prefer to seize on the opportunities at hand, and buy some time off for the following year? The group were swayed; they would get on with the job.

Joe Boyd claims he was unaware of these internal problems – "They seemed to be a very well-balanced, well-adjusted group of rock 'n' rollers, and have a very healthy and positive approach to what they did" – but was concerned about having the freedom to produce.

"There were certain tracks where I felt more involved because there were outside musicians," he says. "The fact that there was this outside element injected into it meant that it was less producing a group, and more like producing a record. And for that reason, I felt much more in control of those three tracks, and ultimately was the happiest with those. And I guess my main disappointment with the record was not achieving on the other tracks the same impact."

The sessions were not completely soul-destroying. For outtakes and B-sides, the group recorded their mock metal anthem 'Burning Hell', a cover of Pylon's 'Crazy', 'Bandwagon', and a brooding song that had been showing up in their live set, 'Theme From Two Steps Onward'. Perhaps fittingly though, the tape of the last of these, fully mixed and complete with saxophone overdubs, was lost – it is presumed to be somewhere in London – along with an acoustic version of 'Driver 8'.

Once it left the recording stage, the album got even harder. Boyd's continual search for the ideal mix came as a shock to a group used to reeling them off like so many demos; conversely, the producer found their musical modesty of no assistance. "With most bands," he recalls, "everyone's saying 'I can't hear my guitar, or my voice. Turn it up, push it up louder.' With R.E.M. everyone was saying 'No, there's too much of me in there, pull it down.' "

■   ■   ■

■ (James Herbert)

■ (James Herbert)

Looking back on the internal crisis, homesickness and loss of vision that was R.E.M.'s time in London, Michael Stipe concluded that "The result of that overriding environment is the record, which is dark, dank and paranoid."

"It's the most tense record we've ever made," says Peter Buck. "And if you take the stance that a record's supposed to show where a band is at, that does it perfectly."

'Fables Of The Reconstruction Of The Fables', to give the album its full cyclical title, did indeed capture the mood of the R.E.M. that made it. The tension and misery was obvious from the opening song 'Feeling Gravitys Pull', wherein Boyd's string arrangement tugged at the melody from enough different directions to produce a discordant effect that thrilled some and horrified others – Bill Berry among them.

'Fables', as it is most commonly known, was full of surprises and extremes. 'Can't Get There From Here', with its stomping Stax-styled brass accompaniment, 'Driver 8' and 'Life And How To Live It' were all possible single material; 'Green Grow The Rushes' and 'Wendell Gee' – on which Buck played banjo – demonstrated again the group's penchant for tenderness. Yet the album frequently meandered. Occasionally, as with 'Old Man Kensey', this could be interpreted as subtlety; 'Kahoutek' (spelled 'Kohoutek' on the label) could only be described as ponderous.

Lyrically, the album was another progression for Michael Stipe, as the 'Fables' half of the title clearly indicated. 'Old Man Kensey' was written about a real-life dog kidnapper who used his ransom rewards to get drunk, and 'Wendell Gee' was inspired by a family of Gees who all owned small businesses in Athens.

"That's Michael's storytelling record," says Peter Buck. "There's a whole other side to the south: it's the last place where the old tradition really exists. People pass stories down. Being a good storyteller is something that people are known for." On tour that year, Michael would frequently introduce these songs with long and entertaining monologues – or fables.

But what then was the 'reconstruction'? While the title 'Reconstruction Of The Fables' could apply to the group's storytelling ability, or to an examination of their myth, its reverse title 'Fables Of The Reconstruction' seemed a pointed reference to the Reconstruction of the defeated South by the North after the American civil war. Though R.E.M. wanted to redress the image of Southern rock, they felt no need to apologise for their roots.

"The Southerner," said Buck, "is the terminal outsider. In movies and on TV, the Southerners are always hicks. They're idiots. Everyone always tends to look at you as if it's a miracle that you're a normal person from the South."

"It's a very wistful, nostalgic thing," said Mike Mills when asked to draw the correlation between the South and R.E.M.'s new album. "Like trains – when you think of trains in the night, that tugs at your heart a bit... The songs remind me of sitting in your room, fixing to go to bed, and hearing a train a few miles off."

"There's more of a feeling of place on this record," said Buck, "a sense of home and a sense that we're not there."

These emotions were best expressed on the delightful 'Driver 8', with its line "We can reach our destination, but it's still a ways away." Stipe described this 'destination' as "something that's almost unobtainable, it's almost an idea, almost this fantasy or this dream, and you're fooling yourself into believing that it's almost obtainable, when in fact it really isn't."

Such an idea perhaps described R.E.M.'s journey to date, a quest for a Holy Grail they could never quite visualise, and would probably never attain. Yet, like mice on a spinning wheel, they were resigned to spend their entire working lives struggling to find it.

Admitting such uncertainty of direction led to an understandably restrained reaction by the American press, who had been so taken with the bristling self-confidence of R.E.M.'s earlier records. 'The band sound predictable, stalled,' said *Record*; 'R.E.M. don't aim for much more than enigma' complained the *Village Voice*; 'murk' and 'boredom' were two of *Creem's* less enthusiastic adjectives.

But this mooted response mattered little now that the group had secured so large a following, and even less when American rock radio jumped on 'Can't Get There From Here' with a long overdue enthusiasm. The video for the single – itself based on a favourite phrase of Michael's and focusing on the small town of Philomath, Georgia – was as great a step towards commerciality as the song itself, a crazed trip to the drive-in movie starring Mills' and Berry's recently-purchased old cars, plenty of self-effacing comic acting from the group and Jefferson Holt, and even the occasional sighting of the song's lyrics. It too received more play than its predecessors. And although 'Can't Get There From Here' showed absolutely no signs of becoming a bona fide hit single, the album roared into the top thirty, its sales quickly overtaking 'Reckoning''s 250,000 mark. R.E.M. were still travelling inexorably forward.

Yet 'Fables' is rarely viewed with great fondness. Joe Boyd expresses relief "that from the professional point of view it fulfilled its function in terms of sales, so everybody can say it's a success, but I know the group doesn't like it. And that's obviously a source of disappointment to me. We got along very well while making the record, but I think they couldn't wait to get out of England, and basically look on it as a sort of aberration. I was trying to enjoy the role of employee, and ended up disappointed that I didn't satisfy my employers."

■   ■   ■

■   **The video for 'Can't Get There From Here' found the group at last coming to grips with the medium.** (Tom Sheehan)

(Tom Sheehan)

In 1984, R.E.M. shouted from the rooftops the existence of a vibrant alternative American music scene. In 1985, the media caught up and acknowledged them for spearheading this 'movement', while the industry, having learned the hard way that the British pop they had been so avidly pushing had only a short lifespan, finally woke up to the homegrown talent. The Replacements, Hüsker Dü, Guadalcanal Diary, and Green On Red were all signed to big record companies; independent labels like Slash got major licensing deals. The British were equally enthusiastic: in April of '85, Peter Buck adorned *Melody Maker*'s front cover to announce a four-part 'State Of The Union' American rock special, and Island Records even signed California's The Long Ryders direct to their London based label.

■ (Tom Sheehan)

Although it was commonly referred to as one, R.E.M. were anxious to prevent the term 'movement' being bandied around. "It is really just a bunch of musicians who worked out their own philosophies all across the country," said Michael Stipe. "It was only after we started travelling and met each other that we began to see we had all these things in common."

A loose affiliation of groups or a movement, the underlying philosophy was to follow one's own instincts and refuse to accept the myth that the industry knew better. "One of the most gratifying things we could do," said Peter Buck in '85, "would be to prove that you can become successful on your own terms. You don't have to submit to all the business crap. They tell you you have to dress real flashy and be real showy and open for the big bands and take the usual routes to success. And that's just not true – just because it works for some people doesn't mean it works for everybody."

Yet those underground acts who rushed into the arms of major labels at the first opportunity came up against these attitudes time and time again. The dilution of their ideas and music by corporate America ultimately proved enough to take the sting out of whatever movement may have existed. It was only those bands whose record labels gave them some leeway, such as R.E.M. with I.R.S. (who had now switched their manufacturing and distribution from A&M to MCA), who could really carry the ethos through.

Not that one would know it from R.E.M.'s comments. Referring to 'debacle' of The Police support slots, Bill Berry pronounced that "Our intuition has been more valuable to us than any of the great words of wisdom passed on to us by the damned record company."

It is the record company's burden to be the bane of a group's existence: every suggestion made to increase the band's profile is viewed as an attempt at coercion, every box of unsold albums as a failure. R.E.M. walked a thin line with I.R.S., getting their own way on a company that loved the band yet was frustrated by its seemingly deliberate obscurity.

"I think a major label would have dropped them," says Miles Copeland of R.E.M. "Because they weren't prepared to make the normal concessions that people would expect, i.e. coming up with a single. Major labels just don't have the time to bother with an act that takes a long time to build."

Not that the I.R.S. supremo didn't try the major label approach himself. Early on, he sat them down and, as Bill Berry recalled, told them that "We didn't have the image, we should be going on all these monstrous tours opening for people all over the world, we should do this, we should do that, we should have a big-name producer, we should make high-tech videos..."

The band replied that they wanted to do it their own way. "I said, 'Well then you have to pay the price of those decisions'," recounts Copeland. " 'You can't expect us to give you a number one single if we don't think that there's one there', and they said 'Well, we're prepared to pay that price'. And the surprising thing – and the thing that I will always respect them greatly for – is that when the albums didn't have a number one single, they didn't come back and say, 'Well where is our number one single?' They lived by the rules that they set."

"I want to make my own mistakes," comments Peter Buck. "We just figured we knew what we were doing more than anyone else in the world. I took advice from Jay, I took advice from my girlfriend, I took advice from my dad . . . I listened to it anyway. Didn't always do it. We'd never do anything against our will. We almost felt we had to be in creative control, because if you make a record and someone butchers it or forces you to do something you don't wanna do, there's no reason to make it. You might as well go back and work in the garage for someone else, taking orders."

This confrontational attitude would have spelled disaster at many record labels. Fortunately Jay Boberg, who Miles Copeland appointed President of I.R.S. in March 1985, understood the appeal of their way of thinking.

"My relationship with them was never to *tell* them what to do, in the classic A&R-record company-band relationship," says Boberg. "It was always this pot-pourri of ideas. The band were the ultimate arbitrator. They would never come back and say 'Yeah, what a great idea, we're going to do it', it would just be that they would slowly grasp the concept, and then implement it at their own pace."

In working as such a self-reliant unit, R.E.M. were more than merely lucky to have the services of Jefferson Holt and Bertis Downs. It is quite likely they would never have been the success they became without these two perfectly complementary managers fighting for them at every turn.

"So many bands, try as they might, never hook up with the right people," says Mitch Easter, familiar with this dilemma himself. R.E.M. "are so lucky to have those two guys. I'm not aware of any mistake either of them has made. Jefferson is the greatest, because he's got this goofy persona, but you can tell he's smart. His mum was a politician, he went to Oxford, he's this educated guy who likes to act like the world is ridiculous and he's just totally boggled by it, and you know he's not boggled by it at all, he's actually really sharp."

Although he did not become their manager overnight, there seems little doubt that Holt aspired to that role from the moment R.E.M. first captivated him in North Carolina. He was partly helped by his own multi-faceted character being a pivot around which the group members' own disparate identities could revolve. "He was a Godsend," says Kathleen O'Brien. "Jefferson was the only personality I think that each individual in the band could relate to."

And while there were other people early on who expressed an interest in being involved – O'Brien, Jonny Hibbert, David Healey – none of them could prove their devotion and suitability like Holt. For example, says Sandi Phipps, who worked in the R.E.M. office until 1987, while both Holt and Healey were known for ebullient behaviour, it was the former who "knew to reserve himself and dedicate his total energy and focus to (R.E.M.). And that's what they wanted."

The only person he would let into the structure was Bertis Downs, who became ever more involved once R.E.M. were on I.R.S. "He needs Bert," says Sandi, "because Bert has a legal background. He's really the brain in a lot of ways behind making it happen. Because of that trust that began a long time ago, he's always been number two."

■ **Jefferson Holt** (Caryn L. Rose)

Jefferson Holt is legally and artistically R.E.M.'s fifth member, accompanying them on tour, making appearances in videos, getting namechecked in songs and running Michael Stipe a close second in changes of image. Bertis Downs IV, to preserve his status as an attorney, takes only a fee from R.E.M./Athens Ltd, although he does get a share of publishing equal to Jefferson's. Everybody else in the office is, noticeably, female.

■ **Geoff Trump.** (Sandra-Lee Phipps)

"They were always adamant that I was a secretary – and paid that way," says Sandi, who stresses that while her role was always much greater than that, chauvinistic attitudes blurred the group's vision to the point that she finally left. A group that spends so much time on the road – which is the biggest Mens Club of them all – is bound to maintain a loyalty to their own sex. But R.E.M. are nothing if not loyal, running their live operation with the same steadiness as their recording career. Chris Edwards, their security man, was a co-owner of Tyrone's; and Geoff Trump, their English-born tour manager, has been with them since 1984; in turn, Curtis Goodman; their chief roadie who died of cancer in 1987, refused to stop working with them until he was too sick to do otherwise.

That R.E.M. have never lost money on tour – even when that meant staying five to a hotel room – again speaks highly of Jefferson and Bert. "You've got two unique and special individuals there," says Jay Boberg. "It's interesting how they play off each other: Jefferson would be really mad

■ **Curtis Goodman, R.E.M.'s first, most devoted roadie.**
He died of cancer in late 1987. (Sandra-Lee Phipps)

about something, and then Bert would call me up the next day and be buddy-buddy. I'm not saying it was good cop-bad cop, but it definitely was a tandem."

Holt and Downs like to present themselves as 'hands-off' managers. Their job, says Downs, "is relatively easy, because the band manage themselves. They're involved in business decisions, delegating very little of their career to other people. They really don't count on us for all that much judgement."

This is true. R.E.M. – despite being college drop-outs – have always been one of the most organised groups in existence. Early on, they agreed to operate as a unanimous democracy, whereby all proceeds would be equally shared, and one strongly opposed person could veto an idea. Although they fight and argue, they believe in giving each other their own space. When the occasion arises, R.E.M. close ranks and enter into serious conference meetings that only Holt, and nowadays Downs, is privy to. Their understanding of the business world, says Sandi Phipps, is such that "they always paid the corporate dues before anyone else got any money."

But this should not detract from the skills of a management duo adept at recognising opportunities, enthusing record companies, and tempering an image of the easiest-going band in the world – one responsive to charity requests and prepared to cut the losses with promoters on bad nights – with a voracity for the best deal possible.

"Dixon and I fought to get more money out of them," says Mitch Easter of his production fees in those days. "We couldn't get it. I had to admire Jefferson. He's just like a rock. And we didn't dislike him at the end of it either. That's what a manager has to do."

■ ■ ■

After successfully hoodwinking The Uptown Lounge in Athens into booking them as a promising out-of-town band called Hornets Attack Victor Mature, R.E.M. then made the tour of colleges during the peak spring party season of late April and early May '85 that their album's recording had been worked around. 'Fables' would not be out until June 10, but the group's enormous popularity on campus gave them the opportunity to break in new material on enthusiastic audiences, and the fee of around $12,000 a night put money in the bank for the rest of the year.

■ **Hornets Attack Victor Mature, aka R.E.M., at the Uptown Lounge, Athens, in the spring of 1985.** (Sandra-Lee Phipps)

■ **Athens, summer 1985.** (Tom Sheeha

June found them back in Europe. While the American press had cut back their praise when it came to judging 'Fables', their British counterparts were proving uncharacteristically faithful. But the front covers and general ballyhoo counted little when R.E.M. accepted U2's personal invite to support them at huge outdoor shows – their first since The Police dates. Like that day at Shea Stadium two years before, it was raining torrentially when R.E.M. took the stage at Milton Keynes Bowl on June 22, coming on just before the headliners. The 50,000-strong crowd was in no mood for a band opening a set with as downbeat a song as 'Feeling Gravitys Pull', and the group spent the entire set dodging missiles, the most common of which were plastic bottles full of urine. R.E.M. went on to play other major European festivals in Ireland and Belgium to friendlier responses, filling the time in between with club dates.

Back in the States, their popularity varied enormously region by region. In Milwaukee on August 5, they played to 1100 people in a hall built for almost four times that many; the next night in Chicago, they played to a phenomenal 6000 avid fans. Their increased success was bringing with it a dubious new audience, however.

In Ottawa on August 17, playing a 500-capacity club after weeks in halls up to ten times that size, they were greeted like conquering heroes, despite the fact that they were drunk, tired, and as far as they were concerned, playing by rote. As a result, Michael Stipe broke into his beloved acappella version of 'Moon River' half way through the set.

■ **On tour in 1985, Michael Stipe frequently went on stage with yellow hair. The dye he used? Mustard.** (Sandra-Lee Phipps)

A lone, harsh cry of 'Fuck Off!' bellowed forth from the crowd. Once Mike Mills was restrained from attacking the heckler ("You come up here and fuck off!") Stipe began the song again, was still heckled and at the end of it was met with calls for 'Catapult' and 'So. Central Rain'.

Frustrated with themselves and their audience, the group played only three more of their own numbers all night. Instead they covered songs as perverse as The Sex Pistols' 'God Save The Queen' and Lynyrd Skynyrd's 'Sweet Home Alabama', as old as 'Paint It Black' and 'Secret Agent Man', and as ridiculous as 'The Lion Sleeps Tonight' and 'Smokin' In The Boys Room'. It ended as one of the most enjoyable nights of the tour, a triumph of the band's convictions, and a bold statement that no degree of commercial success would dictate that they perform a set-by-numbers.

Similarly volatile emotions were displayed when the group played New York that year. On August 31, the first American leg of the tour ended with a sold-out show to nearly 6,000 people at Radio City Music Hall, one that was enjoyable if uneventful until, during an encore of 'Windout', Peter Buck suddenly, inexplicably threw his new Rickenbacker across the stage and stormed off.

Then on November 9, they performed at The Beacon Theater for the New Music Awards as promoted by the College Music Journal. 'Fables Of The Reconstruction' had become the most reported album in the history of college radio, a medium whose influence had grown to the extent that CMJ was able to attract guests like U2 and Andy Warhol for their awards show, and sell its live broadcast to MTV. R.E.M. were happy to show their gratitude to college radio and to collect their award for Album Of The Year; they didn't, however, wish to be seen performing across the nation's living rooms. It was agreed they would go on stage after the awards – and TV broadcast – were over.

R.E.M. duly played an acoustic set that was among their more inspired moments, including The Everly Brothers '(All I Have To Do Is) Dream', a new song that would become known as 'Swan Swan Hummingbird', 'Angel' by The Neats, and a finale of 'Rockville' on which Mike played piano, Peter Holsapple guitar, and two of the Bangles sang backing vocals.

An electric set followed. But during the third song, 'Can't Get There From Here', Peter Buck's Rickenbacker was seen flying through the air to exit stage left while its owner disappeared stage right. The show was evidently over. An apologetic Michael Stipe returned to sing 'Moon River' before the entire group congregated backstage for a fully-fledged row.

It transpired that the sound crew, hired for the television broadcast, felt that their job was done when the broadcast finished. "Nobody could hear anything," recalls Buck of the electric set. "I went over to the guy and said 'The monitors aren't working'. He said, 'Hey! I'm off work', so I said 'Fuck you!', took my guitar and threw it at him. It was like, 'If we're supposed to be such big guests at this thing, and they're not going to bother to even turn the monitors on, I'm not going to play'."

The incident was duly blown up by the music media to significant proportions. Certainly it was an unprofessional outburst at such a prestigious event, but that was the last of Buck's concerns. It was not merely ironic that he considered it more important to finish a show at an air force base in Texas – where he had berated Bill Berry for the same actions – than at an awards event in New York. It was a clear statement that the music industry disgusted him as much as ever.

It was also probably the act of someone who had used the time spent waiting to play to get uproariously drunk. R.E.M. have never been slouches when it comes to boozing, and Peter Buck has readily admitted he spent much of 1985 in an alcoholic haze.

Michael Stipe spent it confounding people's expectations with an ever-changing array of increasingly bizarre images. The golden curls that had grown over 1983 and '84 were shorn at the beginning of '85 for a monk's tonsure and an Abraham Lincoln-styled beard. That was followed by shaving his entire head, eyebrows included, and then by dying the new growth with peroxide. In late October he took to a Glasgow stage wearing watches all over his body and with the word 'DOG' written in felt tip across his forehead. As he began sweating in the heat of the show, and the ink dripped down his face, the audience was inclined to believe his sanity was slipping away with it.

He was sick, he admitted later, but not mentally. "I couldn't stand up. I hadn't eaten anything but potatoes for a whole week 'cos the food is so bad in England. I was vomiting and

shitting. I felt like a dog so I took a felt tip and wrote it across my face."

That British tour ended with two nights at London's 3500-capacity Hammersmith Palais. The British capital was not far behind New York in terms of the band's live appeal, but nationwide commercial acceptance seemed as distant in the UK as it seemed close in the US. I.R.S. had released 'Wendell Gee' as a single with incentive bonus tracks – including, at last, the vastly underrated 'Ages Of You' – and the group again appeared live on *The Tube*, but album sales were not justifying the expense of touring the UK, money that was coming out of R.E.M.'s pockets.

"We couldn't get arrested," says Jay Boberg bluntly of the label's attempts at airplay in the UK. "We tried: we tried 'Talk About The Passion', we tried 'Wendell Gee', we tried fucking everything. They had this hard core following, but it just stopped there. You hit a wall. (R.E.M.) felt frustrated by it. In Europe, with CBS International (who licensed I.R.S. product there), I don't think they felt the kind of energy, so they just said 'Fuck it'."

It would be two years before R.E.M. would venture back to Europe. The renewed interest in American rock subse-quently ground to a halt in fad-conscious Britain. But enthusiasm for R.E.M. remained. And the group that finally returned would be a much happier one than that which decided that three months a year spent away from their American homeland was three months not worth it.

■ ■ ■

■ **Early 1985 found Michael Stipe playing with his image, shaving the top of his skull and growing a Lincoln-styled beard.** (Tom Sheehan)

Athens at the beginning of 1986 was an even greater center of activity than usual, with a film crew in town documenting what was now a legendary scene. 'Athens, Ga – Inside/Out' should have been a cause for celebration – acknowledgement by Hollywood of a city like no other – but it brought out a competitiveness unimaginable five years previous. Jim Herbert, who was hired as Director of Photography, recalls how it "caused so much antagonism: bands that didn't get in, bands that feel they didn't get shown the way they thought they were going to get shown. . ."

R.E.M. were above having to worry about such matters. They contributed two songs to the film and soundtrack, '(All I Have To Do Is) Dream' and 'Swan Swan H'. Although, as a documentary, it was not supposed to have any 'stars', Michael Stipe's influence over the film was apparent in the inclusion of so many of his favoured primitive artists; his charisma outshone that of any other front man or woman among the bands featured; and his ever-changing visage – his painted eyebrows and dyed hair – threatened to steal the show. As a film, 'Inside/Out' was an excellent portrayal of a unique community, and was warmly received wherever an audience could find it; the soundtrack album, released on I.R.S. a year later, (with the Everly Brothers' song 'Dream' mistitled) was a more patchy souvenir. When the Los Angeles film makers departed, Athens attempted to revert to business as usual, but it would never be quite the same again.

■　■　■

Rather than rush into a decision on producers as had proved their downfall with 'Fables', R.E.M. began contemplating the possibilities for their next album while still on tour during 1985; it was Don Gehman's name which elicited the most positive response. Gehman, the man

responsible for John Cougar Mellencamp's expansive sound, was renowned for his direct approach; this sat well with a group who, after the withdrawn pessimism of 'Fables', now wanted to make an upfront rock album. They invited him to meet them as they wrapped up their 'Reconstruction' tour.

Like Boyd before him, Gehman was familiar with R.E.M. only by their awesome reputation; when he got hold of 'Fables', he was disappointed. "I couldn't listen to it," he says. "I thought it was just a dirge." Seeing them play a University in Virginia in December '85, with a bad sound and to a crowd so frenzied that the band performed acoustically to ease the hysteria and crush, failed to clarify his thoughts. "I was intrigued," he says of the experience. "I wouldn't say impressed."

Over two meetings with the band – both of which Michael Stipe stayed away from – he laid out his intentions. "I wanted to make records that were more clearly focused," he says. "That were really what I call records, and not just things that go from one end to the other and you don't know what happened. . . To be able to introduce some production styles that maybe they had never used before on their instruments. . . The idea of being able to hear and understand the words that Michael was saying. I was aware that even if I did that you may still not understand what he meant, but at least you'd have a sense of its presence."

R.E.M. meanwhile, merely emphasised their own desire not to become blatantly mainstream, and in the new year, Gehman flew to Athens to spend a day with the band at John Keane's studio working on their most promising new song 'Fall On Me'. The result, with Michael Stipe's voice to the fore, was convincing; he was hired. I. R. S. in turn were happy to underwrite an increased budget in the knowledge that they would receive a more mainstream record.

■　(L.F.I.)

■ (James Herbert)

■ (James Herbert)

Bloomington, Indiana – where Gehman had helped build a studio at John Mellencamp's home – was a world away from the dampness of metropolitan London, and it was there, during the spring, that R.E.M. congregated. The environment was perfect, Bloomington being a college town not dissimilar to Athens, and the group being supplied with lakeside apartments during their three week stay (the record was subsequently mixed in LA). They were enraptured by these surroundings, and Michael Stipe, when not in the studio, spent all his time either out on the lake or in the surrounding countryside, with pen and notebook permanently to hand.

Signalling their intentions to have fun this year, R.E.M. decided to name the album after a phrase in the Peter Sellers film 'A Shot In The Dark'. Whenever problems befell the band, as they frequently did Sellers' hapless character Inspector Clouseau, they would brush them off with his expression that they were all part of "life's rich pageant". But there were no such misfortunes during recording. Despite Gehman's attention to detail and his insistence on confining the working day to eight hours, the backing tracks were recorded within a week. They had an energy and enthusiasm missing from all the group's recordings but the most raucous elements of 'Reckoning'.

"There was a tremendous amount of creative energy," says Don Gehman. "It just came flying out." On 'The Flowers Of Guatemala' for example, Bill Berry suggested using glasses for added ambience, "and it all happened in one take, three minutes." When R.E.M. asked for a pump organ, the studio immediately found one in the vicinity that had been gathering dust for decades; "things just kind of came to us," says Don Gehman, still somewhat amazed. The organ's underlying grandeur is present on every song except 'Swan Song H', contributing to the spacious mood that the group felt ready for.

"In the past we always tried to stay away from big, booming, stupid-sounding drums," said Bill Berry upon the album's completion. "But as a result, they ended up sounding wimpy and lacklustre. Don gave us a big drum sound, but it's natural."

"Don helped me question why I play at certain places," observed Peter Buck. "If he had done this on the last album, I would have said forget it. But this time we wanted it to be more dynamic."

This new-found dynamism was most evident on the crescendo leading up to the simple but carefully pronounced guitar solo that carried 'The Flowers Of Guatema-

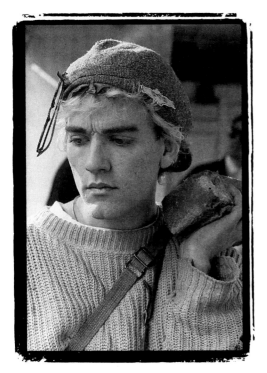

(James Herbert)

(James Herbert)

la'; the overall energy was nowhere more apparent than on resurrected 'Just A Touch', a pseudo-punk rock anthem with first-take vocals that ended in a cacophonous maelstrom as chaotic as any Sex Pistols record.

'Just A Touch' was not the only old song dusted off; 'What If We Give It Away' was a resurrection of a long-forgotten number 'Get On Their Way', and 'Hyena' had originally been intended for 'Fables'. There was in fact a shortage of new material that might have endangered a record not recorded in such uplifting circumstances. The album had to be further padded out with a spaghetti western instrumental to which Stipe added muffled vocals, 'Underneath The Bunker', and a cover of an obscure sixties song by The Clique, 'Superman'.

Originally intended as a B-side, 'Superman' turned out so well that it closed the album and would be a future single, the first non-original song to appear on an R.E.M. long-player and Mike Mills' first lead vocal. It was the perfect R.E.M. cover, the kind of silly power pop epic they might have written themselves in '81 had Michael Stipe continued to pen obvious boy-girl lyrics.

But he didn't. And if 'Lifes Rich Pageant' – or indeed the whole of 1986 – is to be remembered for any significant place in R.E.M.'s ongoing history, it is for the blossoming of Michael Stipe's talents.

The abilities of Stipe will always be a source of debate. To his fans, he is a visionary, a mystical poet unequalled in his era. To his detractors he is merely a pretentious young art student who never graduated. There is ample evidence to support both points of view.

Certainly, as has already been noted, the Michael Stipe at R.E.M.'s formation offered little clue as to his future role in society. Painfully shy and insecure, he could temporarily rid himself of these drawbacks by climbing on stage and singing old rock 'n' roll songs while catapulting across the boards in homage to every great musical performer rolled into one unrestrained 20-year old. On the basis of this, there are plenty of people in Athens who believe that he then consciously *contrived* a mystique around him, that he *created* an enigma; that his persona resembles more the cold calculation of a new David Bowie image than the natural outpourings of, say, a Jim Morrison. This argument would explain his move away from the simplistic lyrics and extrovert showmanship of earliest R.E.M. into the less linear songs and more restrained performance that separated the group from the pack in '82-'83. It would explain,

R . E . M .

■ (Caryn L. Rose)

perhaps, why Stipe swore the few people who knew of his brief existence in a covers band to secrecy, afraid that such a pastime would detract from his image as an outsider and a musical novice.

These detractors claim Stipe's every artistic move to be stolen from those around him: that singing through a megaphone was a trick first employed by The Butthole Surfers, the riotous squalor merchants who spent much time in Athens in the mid-eighties; that de-robing down to another layer of clothes was taken from Mimi Goese of Hugo Largo, with whom he recorded in 1987; that banging a drumstick on a chair was a popular trait of R.E.M.'s old touring partners The Gang Of Four; even the splendid 1986 group promo picture in which Stipe appeared shirtless seemed identical to one taken by a local band only weeks before. Imitation may be the most sincere form of flattery, but at what point, these people say, does it become plagiarism?

This view is then contrasted by those who have always seen in Michael Stipe a rare originality: his painting instructor Scott Belville, or Jim Herbert, who says of the early frenzied performances that many felt derivative, "Even then it looked different. It was an invention. His thing looked like it was coming from some inner place."

Stipe's 'inventions' were tried out not only on the stage, but on a personal level as well. As an art student, there were days when he and his friends would refuse to talk; those who knew him would have to elicit a nod of the head as confirmation that he was undergoing such an exercise. And at Athens parties, if conversation bored him, he would feign a faint, a signal for Peter Buck to drag him home.

His confidant and guitarist evidently enjoyed the process. "People think he's always serious and yet he makes all these weird jokes," Buck said of Stipe in 1986. "He has one of the weirdest sense of humors I've ever seen. It's so weird people don't know it's funny. They think this guy's out to lunch, when in fact I'm giggling up my sleeve."

That humor had been most apparent in R.E.M.'s very earliest days, when Stipe had exerted a playful control over an audience that could have them all crouching down on the dance floor if he so desired. It was also there in his famous animal noises, one of which precedes 'Hyena' on 'Lifes Rich Pageant'.

■ (Caryn L. Rose)   ■ (Ebet Roberts)

The humor remains, most noticeably in Stipe's on-stage monologues. But as he explained in 1988, "Any wife or husband, any lover, can tell you the importance of mystery, what a large part it plays in life, and how important it is to leave a little bit for people to work out for themselves." Working out the mystery of Michael Stipe became a popular hobby among critics and audiences alike as R.E.M.'s popularity grew, and the singer would not always enjoy his placement in the goldfish bowl. While Peter Buck handled growing success by becoming increasingly nonchalant towards it, Stipe attempted to avoid scrutiny by becoming more inscrutable.

When Stipe did crack open the door to his psyche, it was only to admit – perhaps with an element of false modesty, perhaps genuinely – that he himself did not always understand what he was doing.

"A lot of the time I'm grabbing around and bumping into things," he said in '86, "and I'll throw them together and something will come out ... a combination of conscious and subconscious. So a lot of times I figure something out after it's happened: a song, for instance, exactly what was intended. I'm not about to start trying to figure things out beforehand.

"I guess I really focus to detail more than the grand picture, and that detail becomes the words to the song. And given that detail, I guess it's left up to the listener to spot it in and put a frame around it."

It was on 'Lifes Rich Pageant' that Michael Stipe began to put the frame around the picture himself. He was helped by the dramatic improvement of his voice over the years, both on R.E.M.'s records and through various side projects. Most noticeable of these was his participation in the floating line-up of The Golden Palominos, on three songs of whose 'Visions Of Excess' album he sang lead vocals. Coming into 'Lifes Rich Pageant', he felt comfortable at making his voice more prominent within R.E.M.'s often blurred sound. Don Gehman then worked to make its content more tangible.

"Don was the first person that hauled me aside and questioned what I was doing," said Stipe after finishing the record. "That can be really good to have some objective voice saying 'Why are you choosing to say this?' 'Why are you singing what you are?' A lot of the time it was rhetorical, it wasn't the kind of thing I had to answer to, but he would just place the seed for me to think about or change."

"I would sit down with Michael and say 'Well what are you trying to really say here?'" confirms Gehman. "We'd run around the subject four or five times and come up at the same place we started!"

Perhaps it was this friendly battle of wills that inspired Stipe to write a song of intent entitled 'I Believe', only to pronounce that belief to be in 'coyotes', and 'time as an abstract'. If so, it was a rare case of deliberate obscurity, for on the whole 'Lifes Rich Pageant' was Stipe's hour of assertion: "We are young despite the years, we are concern, we are hope despite the times", he assured listeners on 'These Days'.

A political edge was to be found throughout the album, one which often pitted mankind against nature, and, as ever, featured two or more subjects running concurrently within each song. 'Fall On Me', for example, focused first on Galileo's experiments on gravity ("feathers hit the ground before the weight can leave the air") and then on acid rain and the corporations that "buy the sky and sell the sky". 'The Flowers Of Guatemala' ostensibly concerned that country's indigenous flora but also alluded to the United States' imperialism in central America; and 'Hyena', much of which was typically vague, suddenly took on clarity with a middle eight whose lines – "The only thing to fear is fearlessness, the bigger the weapon, the greater the fear" – evidently referred to the threat of nuclear war.

■ **At the Lucy Cobb Chapel during shooting of 'Athens, Ga. – Inside/Out'.** (Sandra-Lee Phipps)

■ (Stephanie Chernikowski)

The masterwork was 'Cuyahoga', in which spring-time swimming in a mud-red Apalachee river was juxtaposed with the rivers of blood of slaughtered American Indians that runs shamefully through the country's history, and an Ohio river contaminated with poison. On top of this, the opening lines "Let's put our heads together, and start a new country up" sounded like nothing less than a call to arms.

All of which was a long way removed from the singer who announced in 1983 that "if you want to talk about politics . . . then you should do it somewhere other than the stage," and in 1984 that "I have no idea what I'm talking about . . . My ideas about how the world fits together are not clearly defined yet."

But like countless bands before them, R.E.M.'s youthful naïvete had turned into a political savvy as they toured the world and opened their eyes to its misery. Michael Stipe's own politicisation was not surprising given his long-term interest in conservation and health foods. He now began acting upon his policy to 'Think Global, Act Local', campaigning during the elections for Congress and turning up at City Council meetings to voice his opinions.

This, noted Peter Buck, was "always fairly strange . . . The things he says in City Council meetings are fairly amusing to say the least, totally befuddling to these old Baptist guys that run the Council."

But they could also be effective. The Congressman he rooted for was elected, and with Bert Downs' legal expertise, some of the Council's attempts to tear down or put up buildings purely for profit were stalled.

As much as 1986 was the year that Michael Stipe came to the fore as a lyricist, spokesman and singer, it was also the year that his role as visual coordinator for the group reached new heights. As a photographer, he had had exhibitions in Athens and Greenville, South Carolina. As sleeve designer, he had made an impact with the colorful chaos of 'Fables'. As lighting adviser, he helped shape R.E.M.'s unusually dark stage presentation. And in the world of videos, he had already taken co-production credits on those for 'Can't Get There From Here' and 'Driver 8'. Now, for 'Fall On Me', he took full control, handing in a promo focused on the ground from above and then turned upside down, resembling the imminent collapse of the sky. As a pointed reference to the commerciality of video – and as

further evidence of his confidence in them – the words appeared on cue throughout.

In 1987, taking his interest in the medium even further, Michael Stipe provided a video interview for use by the broadcast media. "If you were to say that videos are not commercials," he told the camera, "you would be lying to people. The other band members and myself didn't like that aspect of videos, but I've always looked at it as a way of being able to get across the more visual part of R.E.M. And if you can make a video without compromising yourself, without giving in to the look they want, they may never play it on TV, but you've made it, it's there."

The very day that Stipe was working on the 'Fall On Me' promo, Peter Buck was engaging in one of his own favourite pastimes, handling interviews. And videos came in for his familiar drubbing. "The whole idea is despicable," he told *Creem*. "I've never seen a video that made me like a song . . . They all suck. I think it's just a horrible thing that I'm forced to do that shit. Ours, I think, are half-dumb and half-intelligent. I give so little thought to it that I don't really care."

Once again, R.E.M. had cornered both sides of an argument.

■ ■ ■

"We finally got to the point where we could take a little bit of time and relax," says Peter Buck of R.E.M.'s low profile during the first eight months of 1986. Yet relaxation seemed to be the last thing on the minds of a group who used their almost every spare day to work on outside projects.

Buck, Mills and Berry finally reconvened with Warren Zevon. Their performances backed him on most of the singer's comeback album 'Sentimental Hygiene', and it was indicative either of their progression or the record's sterility that at no point did they sound like R.E.M., Michael Stipe joined in with backing vocals on one cut of a record that was an enjoyable experience but a commercial disappointment.

While Michael Stipe recorded with the Golden Palominos and produced Hugo Largo, Mike Mills moved behind the mixing desk for the album 'Hermitage' by the group Waxing Poetics, and Jefferson Holt put plans together to launch his own independent label, Dog-Gone.

Peter Buck, meanwhile, somehow found time to produce two notable albums for Coyote Records, the label for whom he had recorded an EP with The Fleshtones' Keith Streng in the summer of '85 as the Full Time Man. In January 1986, he headed up to New Jersey to produce the long-awaited, and highly acclaimed, second album by the recently reconvened Feelies, called 'The Good Earth'; in June, he and fellow Athenians Dreams So Real travelled to Minneapolis where they recorded 'Father's House'.

Making four complete albums in one year was a feat that even Buck would have a future problem emulating, but it was still not enough to satisfy his craving for rock 'n' roll. So he went back to working behind the counter at Wuxtry, taking his pay in vinyl. It was a sublime situation that not surprisingly he soon found impossible to cope with – fans crowding round him all day long – but Wuxtry reported record takings whenever he did work!

And Bill Berry found time to marry his sweetheart Mary, whom he had been seeing for over two years since finally breaking up with Kathleen O'Brien. He was the first to take final leave of the Mens Club.

■ ■ ■

■ **Peter Buck outside his Athens home during the filming of 'Athens, Ga. – Inside/Out', an obligatory beer in hand. For the best part of a year he walked around town in pyjamas and smoking jacket.**

(Sandra-Lee Phipps)

'Fall On Me' had to be a hit single. Warm, melodic, insistent, produced to airplay standards and under three minutes long, it was the most commercial offering yet by a cult group who were threatening to explode. On the week ending October 4 1986, the song reached the top five of the nation's album rock radio playlists – a notable achievement for a once underground group – and the single entered the Hot 100 at number 96. The next week it rose only two places, the highest it would go.

Top 40 radio was proving resistant until the end, but R.E.M. weren't complaining. The same week the single peaked, 'Lifes Rich Pageant' reached its own zenith of number 21 – a fair placing considering the plethora of major albums released in the autumn – and the group played a 10,000-seater Coliseum in California. In January, the album was certified gold, the group's first 500,000-seller. Hit singles? Who needed them?

R.E.M. spent the months of September through November that year touring North America, consolidating their home country success, and saving loss-making foreign ventures for another year. Those who came along envisioning R.E.M. as reconstructors of the fabled term folk-rock were in for a surprise: R.E.M. were now merely taking on rock itself. Their shows those three months were a powerhouse express, a challenge to the gods of arena rock to match them for emotion and craftsmanship. And the only sign that R.E.M. might fall foul of rock's familiar excess themselves was Peter Buck's embarrassingly long haircut.

As ever, the group's set varied night by night, but it usually started with their new anthem 'These Days' and ended with a melancholy acoustic rendition of 'So. Central Rain'. In between were a smattering of favourites, a handful of suprises and the occasional new song. One of them was a jerking number built around the refrain 'firehouse'; the other was a smoother, more repetitive song with a blatantly mainstream guitar hook and a recurring scream of the word 'fire'. It would become 'The One I Love', and as R.E.M.'s year of optimism drew to a close, it was poised to become a lot more than just another album track.

■ ■ ■

■ **Mitch Easter and Peter Buck check out each other's guitar parts on stage in North Carolina.** (Melissa Manuel)

M.

"Mitch and I viewed R.E.M. more as the Grateful Dead of their college generation than as a hit record machine," asserts Don Dixon of the group he and Easter worked with from 1982 through '84. Perturbing though it might seem to some, there were similarities: by 1987, like The Grateful Dead more than a decade before them, R.E.M. had become the biggest American cult band of their era, filling concert halls and arenas nationwide, and selling over half a million albums a time without the slightest hint of a hit single. The by-product of such a devoted following is always the same: bootlegs.

That R.E.M. should become one of the most bootlegged bands in the world (with over thirty live albums available by the summer of '89) is not particularly surprising. From the outset, they were a collector's dream. Their steadfast refusal to play the same songs night after night, rarely using a set list, playing other people's songs and previewing new material as soon as it was written, meant that anyone who brought a cassette recorder to a show was bound to document a unique experience. The disparity in singles' releases between America and Britain – especially over B-sides – kept the avid fan constantly scouring import shops. And the vast amount of material, such as early discarded songs or album out-takes, never released but circulating on cassette ensured that attaining the complete R.E.M. catalogue was a full-time occupation.

As a result, ardent fans formed an unofficial network by which to swap and collect. Two fanzines – 'Radio Free Europe' and 'Perfect Circle' – sprang up, devoting whole pages to details of a tour's differing set lists or the complete catalogue of available videos. And rare items, such as the Hib-Tone single or the 'Tighten Up' flexidisc given away with the British fanzine 'Bucketful Of Brains', soared into the three-figure price range.

Seizing on this devoted market, catering for the demand of these followers, illegal records began flooding the market. Some of these bootlegs were of genuine historical interest: those first ever demos recorded at Tyrone's in 1980; the RCA demos; and a 1981 live tape from Tyrone's, again recorded on to four-track and widely revered as the 'definitive' early show. Some bootlegs were live recordings worthy for their excellent sound quality or unusual material. And some were complete rubbish, poor quality audience recordings of mediocre performances.

Acknowledging them as a supreme form of flattery, R.E.M. at first actively endorsed bootlegs; Peter Buck in particular discussed their contents with a collector's enthusiasm. In time, the group became frustrated with the bootlegs' increasingly poor quality, but still refused to campaign against them, allowing even the shops around the corner from their Athens office to remain well-stocked with unofficial releases by the home-town heroes.

R.E.M. could have helped quell the demand for bootlegs by releasing a live album of their own, but they have always considered such records a poor substitute for the real event. They did, however, assemble the aptly-titled 'Dead Letter Office' album of B-sides and other gems in the spring of '87. Not surprisingly, Peter Buck took control of this assignment, suggesting in the sleeve notes that "listening to this album should be like browsing through a junkshop." And so it was, with all the delights of unearthing rusty old trinkets that such a rummage entails. Who else, for example, would place three songs by their biggest influence – The Velvet Underground in this case – on one album alongside heavy metal pastiches like 'Burning Hell' and the Aerosmith song 'Toys In The Attic'?

'Dead Letter Office' was the final proof – if any were still

■ (Sandra-Lee Phipps)

required – of the playfulness that so endeared R.E.M. to their fans. Its only weakness was that everything on it had already seen the light of day. A second 'Dead Letter Office', should there ever be such an occasion, might care to dig up some of the excellent, genuinely unreleased material referred to in this book.

Spring-cleaning time that it was, R.E.M. complemented the vinyl B-sides compilation with a home video of A-sides. As well as the group's original choice for the 'Radio Free Europe' promo, there was 'So. Central Rain', 'Can't Get There From Here', 'Driver 8' and 'Fall On Me', along with a half hour of Jim Herbert's rephotography, in the shape of 'Left Of Reckoning' and live videos for 'Feeling Gravitys Pull' and 'Life And How to Live it'. As a collection of some of the era's most uncommercial promos, one might have expected Michael Stipe to use the opportunity to justify his fascination with the medium. Instead, it was Buck and Holt who introduced the mockingly titled 'R.E.M. Succumbs' with the equally derisive promise that "What you are about to see is a representative sample of an outmoded art form."

R.E.M. laughed all the way to the bank when 'Succumbs' replaced Bon Jovi at the top of the best-selling home music videos chart.

■   ■   ■

"The biggest mistake of my life," is how Don Gehman looks back on his decision not to free up the studio time to continue working with R.E.M. Penned in by album projects, he could not offer his services when they came straight off the 'Pageantry' tour and into the studio over Thanksgiving weekend '86 to record an old song 'Romance' for a film soundtrack. Gehman suggested they use Scott Litt instead, with whom he shared management.

A New York-born producer in his early thirties, Scott Litt has a convivial air about him that belies his evident control behind the mixing desk. He came recommended to R.E.M. not just from Gehman but from The dB's whom he had produced while R.E.M. were still playing pizza parlors, and from I.R.S., who surely noted his credits on hits such as Katrina And The Waves' 'Walking On Sunshine'.

Not that these credentials shone through on the result of their hurried two-day session together. The group were physically exhausted from touring, and the song had sounded livelier back in 1982 when demoed for RCA. But the two camps hit it off splendidly, and R.E.M. jettisoned their original plans to continue working with Don Gehman in the new year. In their minds, his meticulously high standards meant that he viewed 'Lifes Rich Pageant' as less than a total success.

■ **Scott Litt at work on 'Document'. He has "a convivial air about him that belies his evident control behind the mixing desk".**
(Sandra-Lee Phipps)

■ (Sandra-Lee Phipps)

■ (Sandra-Lee Phipps)

■ (Sandra-Lee Phipps)

■ (Sandra-Lee Phipps)

"We were talking to Don, but he was getting kinda cold feet," recalls Peter Buck. "He was saying 'I really want to make a record that's a huge commercial success and much as I like you all as people, and I like the band, the way you work I can't hear that you're going to have a huge hit'."

Gehman might have lost out by expressing these opinions. But there seems little doubt that R.E.M.'s first gold album was a useful education: Mike Mills in particular, says Gehman, learned "how to arrange and color" songs from him.

"I felt that I was responsible for giving them a set of tools that worked for them. I showed them a methodology of approaching a song, and production and sound, and they just took the next step. Scott has got a history of knowing exactly the same sort of stuff, and if anything, has got a more commerical background than I have."

Litt, who thought R.E.M.'s early music was that of a band 'a little unsure about being out there', confirms this when he says "I like having a big sound, I like having bold sounds, and I like having a singer that grabs you. I wouldn't accept anything less."

The results of the month spent recording the fifth album in Nashville and three weeks mixing in LA suggest that he got his way, Michael Stipe's clearly-enunciated vocals riding a booming radio-friendly sound on each song. Critics and fans alike subsequently questioned whether the group's continued move towards the mainstream signified their ultimate capitulation to a producer, a calculated decision on their own part, or was merely a natural, unspoken progression.

■ The R.E.M. studio mascots. The 'L' & 'R' indicate on which side of the mixing desk they belong: (Sandra-Lee Phipps)

Scott Litt's comment that "We talked about pop songs when we were cutting the record; they wanted to hear their stuff on the radio too," points to a determination by the group to gain a commercial coating, yet the one issue both parties insist was never raised was the most noticeable: the vocal levels.

"We didn't set out to mix the vocals louder, it just seemed natural," said Mike Mills after the record's completion. "There was a point where we sat back and listened to it and realised that the vocals were clearer and more out-front, but nobody had really noticed it or worried about it up to that point."

It was "certainly not a thing Michael would discuss," confirms Litt. "They would like the sound and they would just go with it. There weren't band meetings about how loud the vocals should be, I'm sure of that. I really think a lot of it has to do with Michael being sure of what he was doing."

Here was something else with which to credit Don Gehman. Having been goaded, pressured and all but physically forced into becoming more audible and focal on 'Life's Rich Pageant', Stipe must no doubt have been encouraged by the response – commercially, in the hefty increase in record sales, and aesthetically, in the favourable reaction of fans to lyrics that closer related to the troubles of the world. For the new album, Stipe took this social awareness a step further.

"The whole album is about chaos," he explained. "I've become very interested in chaos and the hypothesis that there is order within chaos, so I guess that kind of carried over into the recording."

It certainly did on the apocalyptic 'It's The End Of The World As We Know It (And I Feel Fine)'. This was Michael Stipe's own 'Subterranean Homesick Blues', a cataclysmic vision of doom with its tongue firmly planted in its cheek. Among its litany of seemingly unrelated catchphrases and rhymes was a reference to the New York hipsters party Stipe and Buck attended back in 1980 – with jellybeans, cheesecake and a drunken Lester Bangs – throwing Leonid Brezhnev, Leonard Bernstein and Lenny Bruce's names in for effect. Stipe's voice was that of a planet going happily insane.

"I wanted it to be the most bombastic vocal that I could possibly muster," he said later in '87. "Something that would completely overwhelm you and drip off your

■ **Michael Stipe at his desk behind the mixing console in Nashville while recording 'Document'. Note the book on McCarthy.**
(Sandra-Lee Phipps)

shoulders and stick in your hair like bubblegum."

He succeeded, even to the extend of shocking his partners. "It was so quick it caught Peter by surprise," says Scott Litt of the vocal delivery, recalling that the guitarist's first reaction "was that he didn't like it. He was worried that it was such a departure." Only when placed alongside a familiarly stomping R.E.M. chorus – during which Mike Mills played up the song's essentially positive outlook, singing "Time I had some time alone" over Stipe's refrain of the title as if he had not a care in (the end of) the world – was Buck convinced.

Trouble and confusion were themes evident in almost all the songs. 'Welcome To The Occupation' was a continuation – or clarification, considering how vague its predecessors were – of the theme first explored in 'Green Grow The Rushes' and 'The Flowers Of Guatemala', Stipe referring to an imperialistic United States prepared to "fire on the hemisphere below". The increasing power of America's right-wing and the lure of the dollar was also the subject of 'Exhuming McCarthy', with the line "By jingo! buy America!" acidically attacking the regained nationalism of the Reagan years.

"In America, if you can't make money, they think it's because you're a failure," Stipe told *Melody Maker* during

the summer of '87. "The work ethic is really intrinsic to American thought and that has a lot to do with the LP."

No one better exemplified the work ethic than the singer himself. He set up a desk behind the mixing console at which he would be constantly working, either on his lyrics or writing letters to friends. "It made you feel like you wanted to be working too," says Scott Litt. "He was great at just being motivated, and challenging his energies."

When he needed solace, or wished to type without disturbing his partners, Stipe would retire to his vocal booth where the tapping of the keys bled through the

■ **Outside the Sound Emporium, Nashville, where 'Document' was recorded.** (Sandra-Lee Phipps)

microphone with a delightful vibrancy. Their sound was placed at the beginning of 'McCarthy' with little pre-thought, but they came to serve as a reminder of the omnipotent Big Brother, keeping files on one's every move, that symbolised the McCarthy era.

Stipe's work ethic showed up in the reveille 'Finest Worksong', and in the decision to name the upcoming shows 'The Work Tour'. It was Stipe too, who came up with the album's title. As the group mixed the songs to the accompaniment of the film of the 1936 Berlin Olympics, to the televised transmission of the McCarthy hearings, and to other heavy visual experiences, he suggested 'Document'. That, says Litt, is when "everything came together."

The record defined itself both as a document of the latest year in R.E.M.'s life, and as a documentary of the world around them. As such it was able to draw on a wide range of subject matters to make its point. An old Wire song, 'Strange', brought into the live set the previous year and originally intended as a B-side, made canny sense placed amidst the chaos of the first side. A stirring speech by Mother Ann Lee, 17th century founder of the Shakers, an American religious sect who practised celibacy and communal living, formed the lyrics for 'Fireplace'. Athens winos became the subject matter for 'Oddfellows Local 151', and a ramble about 'Lightnin' Hopkins' gave birth to a song of that name.

The lilting sensitivity of 'King Of Birds', as well as being the most successful ballad the group had written, opened up the possibility that Stipe was following the well-trodden path of a star examining his own psyche with the lines "I am the King of all I see, my kingdom for a voice" and "standing on the shoulders of giants leaves me cold". Yet Stipe, as usual, never lets on.

The lyricist also retained some of his cherished ambiguity with 'Disturbance At The Heron House'. Scott Litt, sensing that it read "like a short story", chose to discuss its content with the author – something he otherwise shied away from during the album's recording. "I remember sitting down with him and saying 'This is what it means', going into this long spiel, and he looked me in the eye and said: 'You're right, that's exactly right.' Now that I know Michael, I realise that he could have been bullshitting me – which he probably was!" When, in subsequent interviews, Stipe expressed his (supposed) exasperation at the fact that 'not one single person understood what that song was about', he only confirmed Litt's final assumption.

But the biggest misunderstanding was reserved for Document's centrepiece, 'The One I Love'. The first R.E.M. song to feature pop music's most overused word in its title, it was frequently taken on face value, the opening line "This one goes out to the one I love" suggesting that Stipe was indeed relating a genuine passion. If so, the second line "This one goes out to the one I left behind" was likely a reference to a far-away partner from a touring musician, and the third, "a simple prop to occupy my time", merely acknowledged how uncomplicated these emotions were.

In fact, it was a song of betrayal. "The one I left behind" was someone who had been rejected, cast off. He or she was no more than a "simple prop to occupy" the singer's time, useful only for brief moments of passion. If love had ever been expressed, it had not been meant. Final proof of deception came in the third verse, with the only new line of the entire song stating that "another prop has occupied my time". The singer had moved on to the next object, evidently with no more intention of sincerity than with the previous one.

Michael Stipe, as well as insisting it was not autobiographical, has claimed that the lyric was so brutal he felt reluctant to commit it to vinyl. Even were this true, the sheer emotion of the performance ensured that it would always be a key track. The group recorded an acoustic version to cover all options – in future live shows, they would play the first verse that way – but agreed on the more powerful treatment for the album. On this, each of the three verses began with the same explosively direct guitar motif, each ended with the anguished cry 'Fire!' The result was both succinct and draining. Visitors to the studio would encounter an excited R.E.M. ready to blast the finished track to them from the loudest speakers. "We were so proud of it," says Litt.

■ ■ ■

It had been two full years since R.E.M.'s last European performances, two years of longing by audiences whose thirst had previously been sated every few months. When it was announced that the group were performing a mere four shows on the entire Continent in September '87, stopping off only in London, Utrecht, Paris and Düsseldorf before rushing back to the sanctity of their homeland, the tickets sold out instantly.

At London's Hammersmith Odeon on September 12, R.E.M. opened the Work tour with their first concert in almost ten months, the longest pause of their lives. Suspicions that they would be rusty were dispelled by the opening chords of the just released 'Finese Worksong'; doubts that their UK following might have lost some enthusiasm were proven equally without foundation when the audience sang along to its every word.

Absent from the stage was the Michael Stipe who had appeared so physically sick during 1985, replaced by a healthier extrovert who engaged in amusing banter with the front rows and spun across the stage with an enthusiasm not known since the group's earliest days. Gone too, were the doubtful songs from their fateful album recorded in London, replaced by the energetic anthems of their last two records. Performing under a purposely-askew lighting gantry, they turned the usually comfortable seated confines of the Odeon into a club atmosphere, and responded to the audience's fervor in kind, deciding on the spur of the

moment to perform 'Wolves, Lower' "for the first time since 1983". It was a beautiful mess, guitar riffs going astray and quizzical looks being passed among the performers. How many times *should* the chorus of 'house in order' be played?, they subsequently asked the audience. Three times, as the group had just done, or four, as Mike Mills asserted? 'Chronic Town' had never been released in the UK, but almost 4000 voices roared back the correct response: four. They knew the songs better than the band.

At the end of three encores, the house lights went up and the audience were duly expected to leave. But they didn't. After two years waiting, many simply couldn't bear the thought of another such absence, stomping their feet, hollering and applauding until, several minutes later, a bemused and exhilarated R.E.M. returned to satisfy the hunger, pulling 'Radio Free Europe' out of the mists of time to conclude an unforgettable night. Four shows over an entire continent were not going to sell R.E.M. too many albums, but they did serve to rekindle a few old flames.

■   ■   ■

■ (Sandra-Lee Phipps)

Peter Buck was talking about 'Document's commercial potential just before its release on August 31 1987. "With virtually every record we turn in to the record company we hear outside opinion that 'this is the one that's going to break you guys'. I think at this late date it would be really delusional to even think that's going to happen. Then again I don't care."

The apparently unambitious hero of the underground had been saying pretty much the same thing every year – that R.E.M. and mainstream success were not suited to each other. Sooner or later, he was bound to be proved wrong.

'Document' was received with almost unanimous acclaim – welcome, considering that the brash departure of 'Lifes Rich Pageant' had disappointed some reviewers, but no longer essential: a large percentage of their audience would buy any new R.E.M. album the moment it came out. 'Document' duly charged into the American charts, becoming the group's first top 20 album within three weeks. Which was to be expected, however much Buck hated to admit it. It was even to be expected that 'The One I Love' would become an enormous hit on rock radio – although its writers must have found it somewhat perverse to be challenging Yes, Pink Floyd and Rush for the honour of the biggest AOR song.

What no-one had hoped to expect was that 'The One I Love' would cross over into that last bastion of resistance – top 40 radio – to become a genuine hit single. During October, it did exactly that, a combination of the song's tailor-made radio sound and the surface appeal of its lyrics helping make it one of the most familiar hits of the autumn. Its climb up the singles chart was steady and deliberate until, in the first week of December, it peaked at number nine. That same week R.E.M. received a notable accolade when *Rolling Stone,* which had been so supportive over the years, put them on the front cover as 'America's Best Rock & Roll Band'. By then, 'Document' had also – just – made the top ten and been certified gold, and the group had finished an eight week American tour. It was a short stint, true, but it involved playing to 250,000 people, more than a year's arduous touring could have hoped to achieve four years before.

It is perhaps no surprise that when R.E.M. finally broke through, they did so with such a vengeance. For years, their cult success had been threatening to overflow like water against a crumbling dam, merely waiting for the right song to burst the banks.

"'The One I Love' I always heard as a hit record," says Scott Litt, claiming that he even bet Bill Berry it would make the top ten. "People would laugh, but I never had a problem hearing that record on top forty radio between a Whitney Houston song and something else, the beauty of it being that it's so simple and stark."

Don Dixon says he always believed it would take time – and the right song – to break down radio resistance. "Regardless of what 'The One I Love' sounded like when it came out in 1987, had that come out in 1983 on 'Murmur', it wouldn't have got radio play. They built a reputation for not selling out, not trying to jump on any bandwagon and creating their own thing. So even though not all radio programmers are going to be sitting on the edge of their chair waiting for the new R.E.M. record, all will have enough interest and respect for the band to see what it is they have proffered for their use this time. So many records just don't ever get listened to, where there's not this respected background."

F.B.I. President and R.E.M. agent Ian Copeland agrees that this respect – which he accurately refers to as 'credibility' – is of supreme importance. "It's so fucking hard to get it. Once you've got it, you can go for a lot longer without having a hit record than if you had a hit record and had no credibility – then you're the dead the minute it zips out of the charts."

With a hit single and a top ten album, R.E.M. found plenty of challenges to their credibility – and their peace of mind – at every turn: the bigger, impersonal venues they had often vowed not to play; the money that they had never expected to earn, and were almost embarrassed to possess; the cameras that clicked without asking; the local clubs that publicised their appearance when they dropped in after a performance for a quiet drink or to watch a local band . . . all these they handled with the same familiar nonchalance with which they had treated every previous achievement. Only one issue arose to suggest that the star machine was having an effect on its newest members.

New York State's whimsical 10,000 Maniacs were also starting to taste commercial success during late '87, and their support slot with R.E.M. on the Work tour lent the proceedings the air of a graduation party for the college

■ **Michael Stipe and Natalie Merchant on stage together during The Work Tour. Their close friendship prompted rumors of a romance.** (Ebet Roberts)

buses on the road: one, at Stipe's request, would be quiet, with open windows; the other would cater for the more raucous beer-swilling elements. Similarly, while Buck, Mills and Berry were happy to mill around with friends in one joint dressing room, calming each other's pre-gig nerves with furtive jokes and the odd drink, Stipe sat in isolation in a room of his own, carefully psyching himself up for what was becoming an increasingly theatrical performance. "I'm the odd man out," he explained. "They're all football fans and I'm not."

■　■　■

'It's The End Of The World As We Know It (And I Feel Fine)', released as a single at the beginning of 1988, failed to emulate the crossover appeal of 'The One I Love', perhaps not surprising given its unmitigated chaos. But it did produce one of the group's more enduring videos. Michael Stipe had initially suggested that the entire promo should consist of watching a river go by; fortunately, his proposed director Jim Herbert flatly refused to collaborate on such a non-event and instead suggested capturing the song's mayhem by taking a whirlwind journey through a young boy's room. He found a perfect youthful specimen among the skateboard team Michael Lachowski now managed in his spare time, and the result – shot in a country barn – captured the crazed media assault of the lyrics without trying to allude to their every detail.

radio generation. Each night, Michael Stipe would join Maniacs' singer Natalie Merchant on stage to sing 'The Campfire Song' (as he had done on their album) and soon, Natalie was appearing on stage with R.E.M. to sing 'Swan Swan H'

This mutual appreciation society started fuelling the obvious rumors of romance, encouraged with a wink and a nudge by the British music press. No one actually dared to confirm the rumor in print – which was just as well, as it has never been substantiated – but wasn't it enough that the pair were travelling alone to each show on Michael's private tour bus?

Michael's private tour bus? The notion was as far removed from that of an entire band sleeping together night after night in a rusty old van or one seedy motel room as it was painfully true: Michael Stipe was indeed travelling separately from his companions.

It was not that R.E.M. had grown to hate each other. Far from it. But the differences in lifestyles between the rock 'n' roll band and their hippy singer had grown ever wider, so that with the money now available, they decided to take two

Stipe himself took control for the album's third video 'Finest Worksong' (as with Herbert's production and New York artist Robert Longo's almost sculptural interpretation of 'The One I Love', it was shot the preceding summer). Released as a single in March, 'Finest Worksong' broke the three-singles-off-an-album barrier, and was R.E.M.'s introduction to the world of the extended 12" mix. The addition of a punchy brass section, and the beautiful live medley of 'Time After Time'/'So. Central Rain' on the back gave the fans plenty of incentives to buy it, but again there was no noticeable mainstream success. A 7" version was never even released in America.

Perhaps, for a group within which elements treasured its cult appeal, this was just as well. Even with just one hit single 'Document' almost doubled 'Life's Rich Pageants' sales – as that album had its predecessor – and stayed in the top 40 of the album charts for five months. By January '88, R.E.M. had their first million-selling album.

■　■　■

In the Los Angeles headquarters of I.R.S., the platinum success of 'Document' and the group's long-overdue commercial breakthrough was a cause for both celebration and trepidation. For while it justified the label's faith in the group and their ability to turn a hip college band into one of the country's major acts, 'Document' was the last album of R.E.M.'s five-record deal. The group were now free to sign with any record label in the world – and could name their price.

I.R.S. had frequently tried to stave off this eventuality over the years by offering to 'renegotiate' the band's deal, increasing their royalties and up-front advances in return for more records from the group. Most artists, always eager for as much money in the hand as possible, respond to – or even initiate – such a tactic; R.E.M., much to Miles Copeland's chagrin, preferred to sit it out and wait.

Not that I.R.S. expected the group simply to desert them. The new year of 1988 found the label locked in many public disputes with its artists, but with R.E.M., there had never been a major disagreement. Frequently the group had put their foot down in regard to a finished mix, video or sleeve design, and occasionally the label had insisted it knew better what should be a single, but these were nothing compared to the daily tug of war that exists between most artists and their labels.

"I really think there was a level of communication there," says Jay Boberg of his 'special relationship' with R.E.M. "They were dealing with the head guy in the company. They didn't need to explain many things to me. I knew. They would say 'We wanna do this' and I would just know why they wanted to do it, how they wanted to do it, and how I could go make it happen for them."

Aware that a group almost certain to sell a million albums a

■ (Chris Taylor)

year would be guaranteed complete artistic control by every competitor, Boberg had to hope that loyalty and the aforementioned friendship would win the day. At the back of his mind, he knew that any doubts R.E.M. had about re-signing stemmed from the size and youth of I.R.S. – qualities that, ironically, had endeared the band to the label in the first place.

"A bigger company is more powerful; a bigger company has more leverage in the market," says Boberg. "I.R.S. is a closely-held company. Miles and I are the owners. What happens if I get run over by a truck one day? Then where are they? It was just less stable."

R.E.M., believed Boberg, "felt that great as I.R.S. was, I.R.S. was best at doing exactly what we'd done for R.E.M. Which was: take a baby band, develop them, feed them like a little seedling, give them the space to grow, create that family, and break them. I felt that their analysis was that when it came to take that act from 1,000,000 to 3,000,000 units, there were probably companies that did it better then I.R.S."

The group, while confirming the above suppositions, were most concerned about their almost complete lack of success overseas. This applied partially to the UK, where they found it hard to understand how such a supposedly progressive musical country still excluded them from the mainstream, but mainly to continental Europe and other territories where I.R.S. were licensed through CBS inter-national, a company, the group believed, who neither understood nor cared about them.

"I'll be the first to admit that CBS did not necessarily get the plot in those early days," says Jay Boberg of the years when R.E.M. consistently toured Europe. "But from that point forward R.E.M. only did one four-date tour. So for them to complain..."

■ **Hammersmith Odeon, London, September 1987.** (Cheshire)

"I can see his point, but we did five tours of Europe," counters Peter Buck. In the end, he says, the group started asking themselves "Why are we going to Europe if basically American servicemen come to our shows? (Which, despite their experience back in Wichita Falls in '83, was proving to be the case). If the records aren't promoted? It just doesn't make a lot of sense."

It was this attitude Boberg had to contend with when he attempted to talk R.E.M. into planning, well in advance, a major world tour for 'Document'. It was his best and last chance to prove I.R.S.'s capabilities abroad, and "They came back and said they just didn't want to do it."

"I wasn't sure I wanted to be on the road all that year," says Peter Buck, "when we'd been over there a lot, and spent weeks and weeks and weeks beating our heads against the walls, playing to nobody, and we didn't have that much fun anyway."

Evidently, before spending three months or more out of the year away from home, the group wanted to be assured of positive results. With this and other factors in mind, Jefferson Holt and Bertis Downs duly made the rounds of major labels, narrowing I.R.S.'s competitors down to Columbia, Arista, A&M and Warner Brothers.

All these companies would give the group what they wanted. But Lenny Waronker, the President at Warner Brothers, believed he had three ace cards in pursuing the group. The first was that "We could offer them very strong distribution. Warner Brothers has built itself up over the years to be a very powerful record company," particularly in the international sphere that was so important to the group. Secondly, "You had this company that aligned itself with acts that they all liked – most of their favourite records

came out of this company." A label that had in recent years attracted the likes of Lou Reed, The B-52's, Hüsker Dü and The Replacements, and kept them all reasonably happy, certainly had its attractions. Finally, there was "the fact that we understood the mentality of the band, and wouldn't pressure them to do certain things they couldn't do, aesthetically. We absolutely understood their aesthetic concerns. And at the same time wanted to get them as far as we possibly could get them without interfering with that." In other words, the all-important ability to sell a band without the band selling out: an ability that could only be proven by practice.

I.R.S., aware that the group were in contact with bigger labels, asked to know the ball park figures being discussed to see if they could match them. R.E.M. obliged. Miles Copeland understandably balked when he was informed, as he recalls, that the advances over five albums would break the $10,000,000 barrier, ranging from $2m-$3m a record, the royalties would break 20 points, and R.E.M. would maintain copyright of the masters, leasing them to a major for an agreed period of time. (Copeland believes this period to be ten years; Downs insists "he wouldn't know", but that it is long enough for any label to "make a lot of money off them.")

"The deal was a deal that it was impossible for I.R.S. to make," says Miles Copeland. Unlike a major corporation with its own pressing facilities and distribution, I.R.S. was tied to the details of its own manufacturing and distribution contract with MCA. Copeland was prepared to match the points and advances, admitting that he needed R.E.M. "just for the credibility; even if we made no money from the act, just to have it for our volume was important", but he

■ (Sandra-Lee Phipps)

■ (Sandra-Lee Phipps)

could not offer reversion of the masters when his own deal with MCA did not allow it. Neither could he offer the full royalty on compact discs as Warner Brothers were doing; MCA were among the major labels still paying artists reduced royalties on a long-proven profitable venture.

Jay Boberg says he "worked out a way" to "deal with" the problem of CD royalties, and threw down his own ace card, "the ability to offer them higher royalties on their back catalogue." I.R.S. put in the biggest bid of their lives.

But it was not enough. R.E.M.'s decision to go with Warner Brothers was not financial. "The last thing we wanted to do was to make it an auction," says Bert Downs, and Lenny Waronker confirms that "We never talked about a deal until they made a commitment. They wanted to make a choice based on the qualities of a record company and how they felt the relationship would be, rather than on money. They took a risk in a way, because they made their choice and then negotiated, but I thought that was an incredibly fair way of doing it."

Peter Buck's claim that "We could have got more (money) elsewhere" is therefore very likely true. For a company of Warner Brothers' size, the group's financial demands – which, while nobody will specify them, certainly appear to be close to those discussed by Copeland – did not appear unreasonable. "I don't think that any record company that was involved would have shied away from it," says Waronker.

Negotiating with Warner Brothers was therefore the easy part. Letting I.R.S. down was, says everyone concerned with R.E.M., the hardest group decision of their lives. Jay Boberg was invited to Athens to be told in person.

"It was a terrible terrible day," says Downs, "because Jay to this day is a very good friend of the band's. The thing I finally explained was their having only one career, they had to make the right decision. If they knew they were going to be doing this until they were 60, maybe we would have re-signed with I.R.S. for a few more years and seen what was going to happen. We felt it was the critical turning point, it was going to be next significant chunk of the band's output, and they had to maximize what they were going to do, not only with the money, but their career."

"It was a real hard move," acknowledges Peter Buck. "There's no label in the world that could have done for us what they did. What other label would have been able to get us to where we were, trusted us to give us the artistic control? Sometimes you just feel it's time to move on."

None of which comforts Jay Boberg. "I think injustice occurred, in that the little guy got beaten out for no apparent, no obvious reason," he said almost a year after the dust had settled. "I can't begin to tell you that I'm not still bitterly disappointed."

■   ■   ■

With the financial security of their enormous Warner Brothers record deal, R.E.M. might not have been expected to return to the studio in a rush. But their determination to release an album every calendar year got the better of their initial plans to rest, and while the ink was still drying on their new contract, they entered the studio fully intending to double the six weeks they had spent recording 'Document'.

This they did partially in the knowledge that their popularity

■ **Dusseldorf, Germany, September 1987.** (Cheshire)

virtually ensured the project's profitability – ever since the surprise success of 'Murmur', R.E.M. had recouped their recording costs on the day of an album's release. They were also admitting that they were no longer the biggest fish in a small pond of cult popularity, but a medium-sized fish in an enormous river of mass acceptance, and as such, had to comply to certain production standards.

But the main reason was to offset what they saw as 'Document's one weakness: its similarity in style to its predecessor. R.E.M. derived great satisfaction at making each record a radical departure: 'Reckoning' had been a carefree return to their live roots after the layered mystique of 'Murmur', and 'Fables Of The Reconstructions' tense emotions were offset by the musical optimism of 'Lifes Rich Pageant'. And although 'Document' contained more dark, forbidding moments – particularly on its second side – than its predecessor, R.E.M. were not happy. In their view, by opening albums with ready-made anthems like 'Begin The Begin' and 'Finest Worksong' they were falling foul of their own myth; in embracing such a formulaic arena rock sound, they were becoming too standardised. It was time for a conscious change, one that could only evolve out of time spent in the studio.

Scott Litt, however, remained. In making 'Document', he had become a confidant, an ally and a friend, the first studio partner they felt at home with in three years. As such, he was party to the new approach.

"We had a great budget, we had the time to do it, and there was a group of people that were very close, that really trusted each other, and it was really time to shoot for the stars," he says. "Not really knowing how to do that, except with hard work. We worked. 'Document', which was really effortless, turned into 'Green', which was the hardest effort I've put forth."

With the exception of the somewhat sardonic reference to the color of dollar bills, of which the whole world now knew that R.E.M. had almost too many to count, the title 'Green' was chosen early in the day for its many positive connotations: the group's 'Green' politics, naïvete and enthusiasm. It was, says Michael Stipe, a slap in the face to the 'shop-bought cynicism' of the era. Lyrically, he made a conscious decision to turn the political anger expressed over the last two records into optimism. This could be seen at its worst, as a calculated volte-face to avoid appearing

stagnant, and at its best as a positive awareness of the power he wielded – that if the audience were truly listening to his reasoning, maybe they could reason with the idea of hope as opposed to despair.

The three playing members warmed up to the sessions in Memphis – chosen, like Nashville before it, as a music city within driving distance of Athens – by settling into the rehearsal space beneath the plush offices on Lumpkin Street and picking up each other's instruments. The process was partly an education, forcing themselves to learn to play better the equipment they had often looked at, and partly an attempt to explore the inherent chemistry of the group, to see whether R.E.M. remained R.E.M. even when its characters changed their roles.

When these new lyrical and musical approaches collided, as they did on 'You Are The Everything', the result was the remarkable stylistic change the group had been hoping for. Despite the fear expressed in Stipe's lyrics, the effect was more wistful then melancholic, a love song as he had never sung before. Behind his yearning voice lay a ballad as emotive as the group had attempted, the simple instrumentation seeing Mills on accordion, Buck on mandolin and Berry taking to the bass. It would arguably be the album's highlight.

Michael Stipe, believes Scott Litt, had felt hemmed in by the group's rock instrumentation, and "wanted to start painting some of the landscape himself." With the success of 'Everything', he became more involved in the structure of the music. "'Hairshirt'", says Litt, "started out as just a couple of chords on a mandolin or a piano. Michael would take that tape and come up with the whole verse and chorus, and then we would add the instrumentation after the vocals were done. This was a marked departure from their previous writing. Instead of doing the vocals last, they started doing the vocals first."

'The Wrong Child' – a narrative about a disabled youth gaining acceptance within his peer group – was a further example of this approach. At one point, there was even discussion on making one side of the album completely acoustic, but only these three songs would have fully satisfied the description, and the last two of them, says Litt, would not have been written without the extra time in the studio to force them out.

Indeed, 'Green', as Scott Litt notes, was not an easy record to make. R.E.M. came into the studio with few cohesive ideas beyond the record's two extremes, the acoustic 'Everything' and the stomping 'Orange Crush'. Ostensibly about the effects of Agent Orange and the Vietnam war – although Stipe told at least one friend in Athens that it was in fact about the soft drink orange crush – it was a hangover from the apocalyptic mood of 'Document'. Although it gave the new album its much-needed anthem, it was so close in style to the bombastic stadium rock of U2 that taken on its own, it suggested a frightening new direction for R.E.M. Perhaps for this reason, Michael Stipe sang what might have been construed as the song's chorus through a bullhorn.

It was also to avert claims of predictability and to push themselves forward that the group rejected many of the backing tracks laid down during the session's early stages. Among these were the song 'Title' that had appeared throughout the 'Work' tour and three other numbers that bore all the hallmarks of familiar R.E.M.; in addition a samba called 'Great Big', complete with overdubs and melody, "just didn't fit the tenor of the album," says Peter Buck.

In between the extremes of anthems and ballads, the group found a happy, commercial medium that would dominate the first side of the record. These were songs that Stipe found so pleasurably 'stupid' in their simplicity when presented with them that he rose – or sank – to the challenge by supplying them with equally 'dumb' lyrics. The future single 'Stand', for example, combined one of pop music's most obvious chord structures with a tune of staggering naïvete, direct lyrics, and a wah-wah guitar solo that lent the finished song an undeniable kitsch value.

■ **Green tour, 1989.** (Chris Clunn)

Like the opening number 'Pop Song 89' – wherein Michael repeatedly called 'Hi!' while wondering aloud "Should we talk about the weather/should we talk about the government?" – 'Stand' was as much a comment on pop music as it was a pop song. It could be taken as a clever *satire* of the genre as much as it could be loved by young children for its pure inanity. Once more 'R.E.M.' had all bases covered.

Equally direct in its musical structure was the alarm call 'Get Up', but this at least allowed for some traditional R.E.M. confusion, Stipe singing "Dreams they complicate my life" while behind him Bill Berry echoed "Dreams they *complement* my life". R.E.M. had played with dream imagery ever since they named themselves after rapid eye movement, and now they were openly discussing its effects.

Stipe's willingness to confront his motivation was also evident on two of the album's center-pieces. One, the caustic 'Turn You Inside Out' was recorded during the mixing stages in Woodstock, NY. It concerned the power of the performer, a threatening refrain "I could turn you inside out, but I choose not to do", being met by the object of the singer's charisma promising "I believe in what you do, I believe in watching you". But, as Stipe pointed out, he

■ (Sandra-Lee Phipps)

could as easily be referring to the power of Hitler or Martin Luther King as that of Michael Stipe.

'World Leader Pretend' was less ambiguous and, given that the lyrics were printed for the first time ever, intentionally so. In them, Stipe admitted to coloring his presentation with elements of charade and pretence over the years: "I've a rich understanding of my finest defences" and "I recognize the weapons, I've practised them well, I fitted them myself". Then, teasing his audience like any good rock chameleon – or was it a promise to come clean and be honest from here on in? – he announced that "It's high time I razed the walls that I've constructed ... This is my mistake, let me make it good."

This lyric was less an attempt by Michael Stipe to debunk his own myth as much as a confession that he had created one. This is not mere speculation; in an interview with the *NME* in late '88, he described his image as "an accurate representation of what I put out, which is not of course an accurate representation of me, but those are two different things. I'm aware of the power of it and I'm aware of the ways to manipulate it, the word manipulate being both good and bad. I think I'm aware of how people perceive me."

And to *Q* magazine, he commented that "I know what I'm doing. I recognize when that caricature is getting out of hand and I pull back and I recognize when it needs to go further and I push it."

None of this new-found honesty served to quell the fanaticism with which Stipe was treated by his followers – or Distiples, as they were cynically referred to, a term of derision which applied as much to the small coterie of followers always around him as it did the audience that roared approval at his every word.

In Athens it therefore caused some consternation among those who remembered Stipe as a regular, fun-loving person, when he would deny to the press that he still lived in the town (although he did purchase a sizeable country retreat as well as maintain an Athens residence) or would turn around upon entering bars and restaurants when confronted by a sea of awe-struck collegiate faces.

"I think he just suffers from anything that a person would have with success," says Jim Herbert in his defence. "Egotistically I think he likes it very very much, and in terms of esteem, one of the things artists enjoy is the success, the fame. But I think like most artists, he would like to have the work be better than he is; I think artists secretly would almost sign somebody else's name if they could. They watch through a keyhole as people are in awe. The ego is the awe of the audience. But they really don't want the self-aggrandizement, they don't want to actually have the compliment delivered to them. They're shy of that bit. And they probably don't always receive that bit well."

Ultimately, the inconsistencies within Michael Stipe's character – the early denial of purposeful mystique countered by the later confession of a performer's persona, the supposed approachability confounded by the apparent reclusiveness - are testimony to the inconsistencies within human nature. And Michael Stipe, while a very special one, and regardless of the view of his Distiples, is merely a human being.

The other members of R.E.M. suffered no such dilemmas of ego or fan worship. When Peter Buck attempted to show Bill Berry the drum pattern he intended for 'Green's closing song – with typical perversity, it remained untitled – the drummer was amazed. It was so bad, he said, that it was impossible to play perfectly all the way through. Buck duly held on to the drumsticks and played the jerky rhythm throughout the recording. Despite its hesitant beat, it rounded 'Green' off in soothing style. "This song is here to keep you strong," sang Stipe at one point. R.E.M. had never sounded stronger.

■ ■ ■

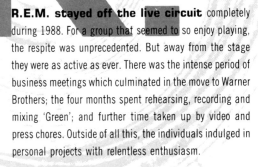

■ (Tom Sheehan)

R.E.M. stayed off the live circuit completely during 1988. For a group that seemed to so enjoy playing, the respite was unprecedented. But away from the stage they were as active as ever. There was the intense period of business meetings which culminated in the move to Warner Brothers; the four months spent rehearsing, recording and mixing 'Green'; and further time taken up by video and press chores. Outside of all this, the individuals indulged in personal projects with relentless enthusiasm.

Mike Mills produced an album 'Sixes And Sevens' for Athens group Billy James. Bill Berry worked with Atlanta singer-songwriter Michelle Malone on her album 'New Experience', and recorded a pseudo-country single 'My Bible Is The Latest TV Guide'/'Things I'd Like To Say', for release on Jefferson Holt's independent label Dog-Gone Records under the name 13111.

Jefferson himself released a record on Dog-Gone butchering classics by Roky Erikson, Procol Harum and Alice Cooper under the nom de plume Vibrating Egg, and the apt title 'Come On In Here If You Want To'.

Michael Stipe teamed up with Natalie Merchant and The Roches to record a delightful rendition of 'Little April Showers' for inclusion on the tribute album of Walt Disney songs, 'Stay Awake'. He also established a close friendship with Michael Meister and his West Coast independent label Texas Hotel, producing the debut record by his sister Lynda's new band Hetch Hetchy for him, recommending other eclectic Athens musicians Chickasaw Mudpuppies and Kid Chestnut, and beginning work on a much-vaunted solo album, 'Field Recordings'. Drawing on a pool of artist friends to help him indulge his abstract musical tastes, the recording turned into a drawn-out process that would hold back its release on Texas Hotel until 1990.

■ (Tom Sheehan/LFI)

Stipe also headlined the summer's Athens Music Festival, performing alongside Atlanta duo The Indigo Girls. Both he and the playing members of R.E.M. then separately contributed to the Indigo Girls' debut Epic album produced by Scott Litt, Stipe providing a vocal on one song, and the band a backing track on another. Proving that they had not yet settled into adult sobriety, the trio turned up at the studio too inebriated to record; they returned the next day to do the job properly.

But all this activity combined could not match the irrepressible Peter Buck. He became an eager sidekick for his former hero Robyn Hitchcock: having played on his 'Globe Of Frogs' album in '87, Buck toured with him during '88 and then brought his distinctive 12-string guitar lines back into the studio for Hitchcock's early '89 album 'Queen Elvis'. He recorded an album with exiles from the Georgia Satellites and Swimming Pool Qs as the Nasty Bucks (named not after him but another member's previous band), played on Atlanta rockers Drivin 'n' Cryin's new album, produced songs for Minneapolis group Run Westy Run, and kept an ancient promise by financing the release of a live album by Atlanta's once-finest, The Fans, on DB Records.

Buck's extra-curricular activities, as producer, session guitarist and a guest star at almost any show he attended was all the more remarkable for having come to the guitar so late in life. This proof that it was never too late to choose a vocation and become a leader in it, along with his modest demeanour and genuine enthusiasm for live music had long made him a role model among the underground, and he was further deified when he became the star of his own comic strip, drawn and published by a local Athens music fan. In it, the caricature super-hero Peter Buck engaged in a quest to preserve the future of rock 'n' roll while knocking back six-packs and stopping off to jam with any creaking

door that he passed by — remarkably like the real-life character. Buck feigned embarrassment at the strip; his credibility continued to soar.

On April 29, however, he apparently waved forever farewell to his rampant past by marrying his girlfriend Barrie, co-manager of the 40 Watt Club, in Mexico. What better bride for a man who spent his every night in bars and clubs than a beautiful woman who ran the best in his home town? That the 40 Watt was now back at its previous location on Lumpkin Street, all of two doors from the R.E.M. offices, formed yet another Perfect Circle.

I.R.S. Records were also busy during 1988. Stung by R.E.M.'s departure from the label at the peak of the group's popularity, they decided to utilise their assets and release a 'best of' compilation. "There was no vindictiveness," says Jay Boberg, but "from a business standpoint, I certainly wasn't going to let that opportunity go away." R.E.M. therefore determined to collaborate on the project rather than be dissatisfied with its outcome.

'Eponymous' was released on October 2 1988 with incentives for R.E.M. collectors — 'Romance', from the soundtrack of *Made In Heaven*, and alternate mixes of 'Radio Free Europe', 'Gardening at Night' and 'Finest Worksong' — along with seven previously released singles and 'Talk About The Passion', for which a new, politically

■ **Extracts from the 'Peter Buck' comic strip, satirically devised by Georgia music fan Jack Logan.**

HE STARTS HIS DAY TENDING TO THE BUCKMOBILE, MAKING SURE THAT IT'S FULLY STOCKED WITH A FRESH SUPPLY OF TAPES. IT'S EQUIPPED WITH A MASSIVE TUBE-DRIVEN CASSETTE DECK WHICH HAS A MEMORY CAPACITY OF UP TO FORTY EIGHT HOURS. SOMEHOW PETE IS ABLE TO CONSUME THEM IN A DAY.

TO KEEP IN SHAPE HE DRINKS A FEW BEERS AND BANGS AROUND ON HIS GUITAR UNTIL HE BREAKS A STRING OR TWO.

uncompromising video was produced. The back sleeve was dominated by a teenage Michael Stipe gazing absent-mindedly from above his mid-seventies open-collar shirt. On one level, this appeared as a further thrust by the singer to the forefront of the group's visibility. On another, it was merely a joke at his image's expense: across the top of the photograph was printed, 'They Airbrushed My Face'.

■ ■ ■

November 8 1988. Across the United States, millions of voters go to the polls to elect George Bush as President of the United States. Across Athens, Georgia, a flurry of music media professionals go to assorted locations in town to interview R.E.M. And across the world, 'Green' is released.

The synchronicity was far from coincidental. Although 'Green' lacked the harsh political tones of its two predecessors, the group that made it were becoming increasingly disgusted with the American way of life. Rather than merely pass comment from the safe distance of a music press interview, both Michael Stipe and Peter Buck gave money to the campaign to elect Democratic Presidential candidate Mike Dukakis, Stipe extending his involvement to the point of placing pro-Dukakis adverts in local newspapers.

R.E.M.'s commercial breakthrough the previous year and the size of their new record deal had served to fuel the expected rumblings of the dreaded term 'sell out'. The music media's annual pilgrimage to Athens for the release of a new R.E.M. album gave them the chance to place the town heroes under closer scrutiny than usual. Could R.E.M. remain the same humble people now that they were recognized on the streets everywhere they went? Could they remain politically active when a mayor they didn't even vote for wanted to give them the keys to the city? Could they still associate with other, struggling bands now that they were one of the biggest industries in the city with a turnover in the millions of dollars?

R.E.M. believed they could. Their humility was preserved, they said, by the fact that here they were hardly noticed, let alone harassed. Outsiders indeed observed an almost wilful refusal by locals to acknowledge the rock stars in favoured hang-outs such as the Georgia Bar or Rocky's Pizzeria. The group explained, in interviews conducted on

■ (Tom Sheehan)

the porch of Peter Buck's enviable new mansion, that once each year's new intake of students realized they could see their heroes any night of the week, they simply left them alone. (Michael Stipe, by virtue of his increased public visibility and image-mongering, suffered the harassment on behalf of everyone.) And if Peter Buck's personal humility was endangered by the size of his house, it was reinforced by his inviting the world to his door to laugh at the perversity of it all.

As for their politics, Stipe went beyond his public endorsement of Dukakis (which carried with it an uncomfortable degree of patronisation), and became even more involved in grass roots politics. Where possible, R.E.M./Athens Ltd. used its clout as a major local business to block conservative council proposals, and where necessary, used its finance: when the city would not back a $5000 study to find ways of preserving historic buildings in a new civic centre design, the group donated the money themselves.

And if their musical contemporaries were jealous or bitter, they didn't show it. R.E.M.'s constant championing of Pylon as a major influence even caused that band's members to consider re-forming, at which R.E.M. promptly offered up their rehearsal space as an incentive. It worked: Pylon became a group once more.

■   ■   ■

It had been widely assumed that R.E.M. would make the easy transition from commercial success to stadium rockers with 'Green'. Scott Litt admits that "So many people were expecting 'The Joshua Tree'," referring to U2's blockbuster album. "And early on I said (to Warner Brothers) 'Listen, I'd like to deliver you a record that's gonna sell 5,000,000 copies, but 'Green' is not that record.' "

In many ways 'Green' was a return to the subtlety of 'Murmur', requiring repeated exposure before its delights could be coaxed out from the mélange of unusual instrumentation or its intrigue unearthed from the directness of its pop songs. American reviewers who could not supply the necessary time instead opted to maul it, just as they would if R.E.M. *had* delivered a 'Joshua Tree'. 'Green' rocketed into the American top 20 but as the new year came round it was at number 15 and slipping, having fallen short of the top ten. I.R.S. were heard to complain that they could have done as good a job. Observers who had calculated that R.E.M. plus Warner Brothers added up to a chart-topping certainty deduced that 'Green' was a disaster.

In fact, 'Green's slow start was part of a carefully-planned strategy between R.E.M., its management, and their new record company. 'Green' was the fourth R.E.M. album made available in only 18 months, and even if two of those were compilations, both had been endorsed by the band. 'Eponymous' in particular, despite Jay Boberg's protestations to the contrary, had almost scuttled the excitement

■ (Chris Taylor)

■ (Chris Taylor)

■ **At home on Peter Buck's front porch in Athens, October 1988.** (Chris Taylor)

■ **Jefferson Hope in front of the 40 Watt Club in Athens.** (Chris Taylor)

building up to 'Green's' release, enticing the casual fans who might then decide not to buy another R.E.M. album for a while, and taking up valuable airplay. No single was released from 'Green' before Christmas (although 'Orange Crush' scored a direct hit on rock radio); after fulfilling their media obligations in November – at which time Michael Stipe even flew to Europe to conduct solo interviews, an unthinkable proposition only two years before – R.E.M. and their management simply took the rest of the year off.

They were all merely catching breath before the most energetic year of their lives. In 1989, R.E.M. would work with the fanaticism of people who had something to prove – which, for the first time since 1983, they did. At the end of January, they would travel to Japan for the first time since 1984 and from there to New Zealand and Australia for the first time ever. During March and April they would tour America and Canada, playing almost without exception the arenas that had been successfully introduced on the 'Work' tour; in May and June they would attack Europe with uncharacteristic vengeance, and after a month or so off, they would make another complete circuit of North America.

The entire year had been planned out as far in advance, and on the scale, that Jay Boberg had begged them to do – and which they had refused – for 'Document'. Although this caused him some bitterness, he knew as well as anyone that the band had been conserving their energy until the time that a major conglomerate could prove its international power. That time was now.

After the two dates in Japan, Australia greeted them as heroes. The audience there knew the entire set and yet were prepared to listen – rather than shout – through Michael's a cappella songs. The Australians in particular were delighted to find so un-starstruck a group and, in a country which takes its beer seriously, one who could drink with the best of them. 'Green' promptly went gold there.

R.E.M. then began their nine-week circuit of America with almost impeccable timing. 'Stand' had been released as a single at the beginning of January and broke into the top 30 just as the tour kicked off. For three weeks in the middle of it – during which R.E.M. played to 27,000 people over two nights in Atlanta and sold out the 16,500 tickets at New York's Madison Square Garden in an hour – 'Stand' rested

■ (Chris Clunn)

at number 6 in the pop charts. Its playful video topped the MTV playlist. 'Green' entered a fifth month in the top twenty, overtaking 'Document's million-plus sales in the process. 'Murmur' was now past the 500,000 sales mark, with 'Reckoning' and 'Fables' close behind. Rolling Stone put them on the cover again. This time they were called 'America's *Hippest* Band', a useful endorsement of credibility for a group charting with their most blatant pop single to date and performing in venues designed as ice hockey rinks and basketball arenas.

The audience at these shows were almost exclusively adolescent, a natural by-product of hit singles. It was apparent that many of R.E.M.'s earlier fans were choosing to stay away these days, cherishing their memories of the band playing half-empty clubs or at the most, packed-out small theatres, when mistakes were routine and impromptu covers a ritual. "That's fine," Peter Buck told *Rolling Stone*. "A lot of people like bands when they're smaller – and I'm one of them." After many a show, he would run off stage, jump straight into a rented mini-van and head for a decrepit local bar to see rock 'n' roll played in the atmosphere he personally craved.

R.E.M.'s concessions to the size of venues were far from predictable. A screen at the back mocked arena rock's routine empty gestures with the message 'Are you ready to rock 'n' roll?' and the assertion that 'It's really great to be in (your city here)'. The dB's having finally split, Peter Holsapple became an honorary member, flushing out the sound on guitar and keyboards, allowing 'World Leader Pretend' to reach its potential and 'Perfect Circle' to become part of the set after almost six years' absence. Bill Berry came off the drums to play bass during 'You Are The Everything'.

But it was Michael Stipe who dominated. A combination of critical praise, growing commercial success and increasing personal self-confidence had served to turn him into rock's most commanding performer. Whether singing with his back to the audience, prone on the floor, standing on a chair or through a bullhorn; whether imitating the childish dance of the 'Stand' video, furiously shadow-boxing, or stripping down to his bicycle shorts and t-shirt; whether singing Hugo Largo's 'Harpers' a capella or dangling the audience on tenterhooks at the finale of the Velvet Underground's nightclub reverie 'After Hours'; whether

sarcastically introducing 'Stand' as a work of high culture or urging his audience to boycott the Exxon Corporation, Michael Stipe was transfixing. Even the fact that his phrases and actions were almost identical every night only slightly lessened their effect, and those who had seen R.E.M. in their earliest days were heard to remark on the similarity between the uninhibited Michael Stipe of yore and the charismatic frontman of now. It was another Perfect Circle.

In Europe, Warner Brothers' international arm, WEA, appeared to be making the hoped-for difference, and therefore it was a minor catastrophe when Bill Berry went down with Rocky Mountain Spotted Fever in Germany. Fortunately, only four shows were cancelled – and subsequently rearranged – and the group moved on to Britain, where there were no such disappointments.

Whether R.E.M.'s absence over the last three years had served to fuel the fires of fanaticism, or whether continued attention to the area would have resulted in an eruption of acceptance even quicker is hard to ascertain; certainly by 1988 – The Smiths having split up, U2 having outreached themselves and nothing of equal potential emerging from a fragile club scene – R.E.M. were the number one choice of rock fans everywhere. 'Green' had been treated by the British rock press with a hyperbole remarkable even by their own unparalleled standards. "The best band in the world? I think so," wrote *Q*; "the world's smartest, most mysterious group in motion," said the *NME*; and Allan Jones, exercising the editor's prerogative to write about his favourite group, wound up a review of ecstatic intensity in *Melody Maker* with the assertion that "they could bow out now with 'Green' and we would remember them with nothing but awe."

'Green' had entered the British charts upon release at an impressive number 27 – quickly to disappear, of course – and R.E.M. had shown as high as second top group in the readers' polls. 'Stand' had then been a near-hit in February and their two-week tour – including two nights at Hammersmith Odeon – had sold out immediately. Now they found themselves adding arena dates; once more they would be playing to as many people in London as New York.

The week R.E.M. arrived in the UK, the *Sunday Observer's* magazine put them on the cover, alongside the headline

'The best band in the world' as if it were beyond question. 'Green' re-entered the album charts that same week on its way to going gold. More visibly, 'Orange Crush' crashed into the singles' charts; it would go top 30 and see R.E.M., the cult band of its era, perform on the notoriously vacuous British television show *Top Of The Pops*. Like America before it, the British Isles had succumbed. Like American fans before them, the British would have to get used to sharing their most prized secret with the masses.

As R.E.M. gatecrashed the musical mainstream world-wide, it was with pleasure, nonchalance, surprise and disdain. They had never contemplated being the best band in the world – they still didn't – but others found that mantle increasingly hard to disprove.

The demands of touring ensured that there would be no new recording until 1990. Peter Buck, the eternal rockist, let it be known that he would like to make a 'real chamber record', dominated by orchestral instruments.

Michael Stipe, the primitive artist, let it be known that he would like to record 'a rock 'n' roll-thrash-pop' album.

The guessing game would evidently continue.

■ ■ ■

■ **At the Buck Mansion, October 1988.** (Chris Taylor)

■ (Chris Clunn)

■ (Chris Clunn)

■ (Chris Clunn)

A hot spring day in Athens, Georgia. A bright yellow sun sits lazily in a cloudless blue sky, observing from its enviable perch the activity below. On Milledge Avenue, fraternity brothers, unerringly uniform with flat haircuts, knee-length trousers and t-shirts all adorning nautilus bodies, jog enthusiastically past sorority houses; sorority girls, equally generic with their flowing blonde hair and chubby, pretty faces, speed-walk past the fraternity buildings. They are all taking part in an elaborate mating ritual, a preening and a pruning of their bodies for the orgiastic week on the Florida beaches during the approaching spring break.

On campus, bronzing young bodies dot the lawn, the occasional text book lying open in front of their closed eyes.

In the heart of town, close to the University of Georgia's entrance, on Collége Avenue and Clayton Street, senior students gather around the cluster of sandwich shops, pizzerias and restaurants to discuss impending exams, future vocation plans, and celebratory parties.

Among them, enthusiastic vinyl junkies tread and retread the ten yard journey between the two major record emporiums, Wuxtry and Ruthless, picking out the latest hip releases as aired on the college radio station, under the watchful eyes of the town's stars, gazing benignly down from posters lining the walls.

At the town's favoured nightspots, the 40 Watt, the Uptown, the Georgia Bar, and the Kingfish Lounge, managers rub sleepy eyes, sweep the floors and prepare themselves for today's visiting bands and afternoon drinkers.

The night people, the bohemians with their rock bands, paint brushes and honorable intentions, rub even sleepier eyes and tumble out of unkempt beds.

No one hurries. Time almost stands still.

■ (Chris Clunn)

■ (Chris Clunn)

On Oconee Street, a church door creaks in the welcome spring breeze. A sofa, its springs broken, basks in the sunlight, beckoning visitors to trust themselves to its uncomfortable arms. Inside, broken plates, burned year books, cracked windows and a ruined oven suggest one last night of wanton destruction before the building's evacuation. A half-eaten bagel on the floor intimates recent visitors; the putrid smell of sewage from the bathroom confirms long-time desertion.

Upstairs, dirty mattresses still lay strewn across filthy floors, silently reliving memories of drunken bodies collapsing on them in the early hours of never-to-be-seen mornings.

In the downstairs bedroom, the closet door is no longer the only entrance to the back of the church; the entire wall has been torn down, linking together the two strange and once co-existing worlds. Enormous wooden shutters slam eerily closed on windowless panes. The sun beats down through a beamless angular roof. The tiny, rotting altar-become-stage is still standing against the far wall. Graffiti is strewn everywhere, its messages carrying the mark of differing youth cultures: 'Rude Boy Romance', 'Walking In The Shadow Of The Big Man', 'Eat At Waffle House', 'The Rolling Stones Forever' and a dominating peace sign. Memories of parties and performances are apparent at every turn; the distant echo of laughter and live music carried in the hybrid of noises whistling through the building.

Outside, so close as to boldly threaten the church's sanctity, a youthful tree blossoms in the welcome onslaught of another spring. As the building next to it gradually disintegrates, the tree appears to be gathering strength for a long and auspicious existence.

History marches on.

■ ■ ■

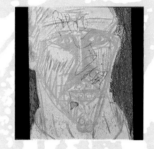

REM DISCOGRAPHY

This US and UK discography of singles and albums features every song that R.E.M. have released. In addition, all notable collaborations and contributions to other records are listed. For reasons of space, however, this discography does not include the many promotional items and variations in each release over the years, nor the individual R.E.M. members' credits as producers. While every endeavour has been made to produce a complete and accurate discography, we will be pleased to receive additional information for future editions.

US 7" & 12"

Radio Free Europe/Sitting Still
Hib-Tone HT0001 (7")   July 1981

Chronic Town
Wolves, Lower/Gardening At Night/Carnival Of Sorts (Box Cars)/1,000,000/Stumble
IRS SP70502 (12")   August 1982

Radio Free Europe/There She Goes Again
IRS IR 9916 (7")   May 1983

So. Central Rain (I'm Sorry)/King Of The Road
IRS IR9927 (7")   May 1984

(Don't Go Back To) Rockville/Catapult (live)
IRS IR9931 (7")   August 1984

Can't Get There From Here/Bandwagon
IRS IRS52642 (7")   June 1985

Driver 8/Crazy
IRS IRS52678 (7")   September 1985

Fall On Me/Rotary Ten
IRS IRS52882 (7")   August 1986

Superman/White Tornado
IRS IRS52971 (7")   November 1986

The One I Love/Maps And Legends (Live)
IRS IRS53171 (7" & cassette single)   August 1987
The One I Love/The One I Love (live)/Maps And Legends (live)
IRS IRS23792 (12")   August 1987

It's The End Of The World As We Know It (And I Feel Fine)/Last Date
IRS IRS53220 (7" & cassette single)   January 1988

Finest Worksong (lengthy club mix)/Finest Worksong (other mix)/Time After Time etc. (live)
IRS IRS23850 (12")   March 1988

Stand/Memphis Train Blues
Warner Brothers 7-27688 (7" & cassette Single)   January 1989

Pop Song 89/Pop Song 89 (acoustic version)
Warner Brothers 7-27640 (7" & cassette single)   May 1989

■ (Peter Anderson)

UK 7″ & 12″

Radio Free Europe/There She Goes Again
IRS PFD1017 (7″)   August 1983

Talk About The Passion/Shaking Through
IRS PFD1026 (7″)   November 1983
Talk About The Passion/Shaking Through/Carnival Of Sorts (Box Cars)/1,000,000
IRS PSFX1026 (12″)   November 1983

So. Central Rain (I'm Sorry)/King Of The Road
IRS IRS105 (7″)   March 1984
So. Central Rain (I'm Sorry)/Voice of Harold/Pale Blue Eyes
IRS IRSX105 (12″)   March 1984

(Don't Go Back To) Rockville/Wolves, Lower
IRS IRS107 (7″)   June 1984
(Don't Go Back To) Rockville/Wolves, Lower/9–9 (live)/Gardening At Night (live)
IRS IRSX107 (12″)   June 1984

Can't Get There From Here/Bandwagon
IRS IRM102 (7″)   July 1985
Can't Get There From Here/Bandwagon/Burning Hell
IRS IRT102 (12″)   July 1985

Wendell Gee/Crazy
IRS IRM105 (7″)   October 1985
Wendell Gee/Crazy/Ages Of You/Burning Down
IRS IRMD105 (7″ double pack)   October 1985
Wendell Gee/Crazy/Driver 8 (live)
IRS IRT105 (12″)   October 1985

Fall On Me/Rotary Ten
IRS IRM121 (7″)   September 1986
Fall On Me/Rotary Ten/Toys In The Attic
IRS IRMT121 (12″)   September 1986

Superman/White Tornado
IRS IRM128 (7″)   March 1987
Superman/White Tornado/Femme Fatale
IRS IRMT128 (12″)   March 1987

It's The End Of The World As We Know It (And I Feel Fine)/This One Goes Out (live)
IRS IRM145 (7″)   August 1987
It's The End Of The World As We Know It (And I Feel Fine)/This One Goes Out (live)/
Maps And Legends (live)
IRS IRMT145 (12″)   August 1987

The One I Love/Last Date
IRS IRM146 (7″)   November 1987
The One I Love/Last Date/Disturbance At The Heron House
IRS IRMT146 (12″)   November 1987

Finest Worksong/Time After Time etc. (live)
IRS IRM161 (7″)   April 1988
Finest Worksong (lengthy club mix)/Finest Worksong/Time After Time etc. (live)
IRS IRMT161 (12″)   April 1988

The One I Love/Fall On Me
IRS IRM173 (7″)   October 1988
The One I Love/Fall On Me/So. Central Rain
IRS IRMT173 (12″)   October 1988

Stand/Memphis Train Blues
Warner Bros W7577 (7″)   January 1989
Stand/Memphis Train Blues/(The Eleventh Untitled Song)
Warner Bros W7577T (12″)   January 1989

Orange Crush/Ghost Riders
Warner Bros W2960 (7″)   May 1989
Orange Crush/Ghost Riders/Dark Globe
Warner Bros W2690T (12″)   May 1989
Orange Crush/Ghost Riders/Dark Globe
Warner Bros W2960CD (CD)   May 1989

Stand/Pop Song '89 (acoustic version)
Warner Bros W2833 (7″)   August 1989
Stand/Pop Song '89 (acoustic version)/Skin Tight (live)
Warner Bros 2833T (12″)   August 1989
Stand/Pop Song '89 (acoustic version)/Skin Tight (live)
Warner Bros W2833CD (CD)   August 1989

ALBUMS (US & UK)

Murmur
Radio Free Europe/Pilgrimage/Laughing/Talk About The Passion/Moral Kiosk/Perfect
Circle/Catapult/Sitting Still/9–9/Shaking Through/We Walk/West Of The Fields
IRS SP7064   April 1983 (US)
IRS SP7064   August 1983 (UK)

Reckoning
Harborcoat/7 Chinese Brothers/So. Central Rain/Pretty Persuasion/Time After Time
(Annelise)/Second Guessing/Letter Never Sent/Camera/(Don't Go Back To) Rockville/
Little America
IRS SP70044   April 1984 (US)
IRS IRSA7045   April 1984 (UK)

Fables Of The Reconstruction
Feeling Gravitys Pull/Maps And Legends/Driver 8/Life And How To Live It/Old Man
Kensey/Can't Get There From Here/Green Grow The Rushes/Kohoutek/Auctioneer
(Another Engine)/Good Advices/Wendell Gee
IRS IRS5592   June 1985 (US)
IRS MIRF1003   June 1985 (UK)

Lifes Rich Pageant
Begin The Begin/These Days/Fall On Me/Cuyahoga/Hyena/Underneath The Bunker/
The Flowers Of Guatemala/I Believe/What If We Give It Away?/Just A Touch/Swan
Swan H/Superman
IRS IRS5783   July 1986 (US)
IRS MIRG1014   July 1986 (UK)

Dead Letter Office
Crazy/There She Goes Again/Burning Down/Voice Of Harold/Burning Hell/White
Tornado/Toys In The Attic/Windout/Ages Of You/Pale Blue Eyes/Rotary Ten/
Bandwagon/Femme Fatale/Walter's Theme/King Of The Road
IRS SP70054   April 1987 (US)
IRS SP70054   April 1987 (UK)
(CD also includes Chronic Town)

Document
Finest Worksong/Welcome To The Occupation/Exhuming McCarthy/Disturbance At
The Heron House/It's The End Of The World As We Know It (And I Feel Fine)/The One I
Love/Fireplace/Lightnin' Hopkins/King Of Birds/Oddfellows Local 151
IRS IRS42059   September 1987 (US)
IRS MIRG1025   September 1987 (UK)

Eponymous
Radio Free Europe/Gardening At Night/Talk About The Passion/So. Central Rain/
(Don't Go Back To) Rockville/Can't Get There From Here/Driver 8/Romance/Fall On
Me/The One I Love/Finest Worksong/It's The End Of The World As We Know It (And I
Feel Fine)
IRS IRS6262   October 1988 (US)
IRS MIRG1038   October 1988 (UK)

Green
Pop Song 89/Get Up/You Are The Everything/Stand/World Leader Pretend/The Wrong
Child/Orange Crush/Turn You Inside Out/Hairshirt/I Remember California/(Untitled)
Warner Bros 9-25795-1   November 1988 (US)
Warner Bros WX234   November 1988 (UK)

FLEXI-DISCS

Wolves, Lower
Free With *Trouser Press*, issue 80. December 1982

Tighten Up
Free With *Bucketful Of Brains*, issue 11. (BOB 5) February 1985

Femme Fatale
Free With *The Bob*, issue 27. (REAL 005) May 1986

FAN CLUB SINGLE

Parade Of The Wooden Soldiers/See No Evil
U-23518M   December 1988

SOUNDTRACKS

Wind Out
Featured on **Bachelor Party**
IRS SP70047 (US)   December 1984
IRS IRSA7051 (UK)   December 1984

Romance
Featured on **Made In Heaven**
Elektra 9 60729-1 (US)   1987

(All I've Got To Do Is) Dream/Swan Swan H
Featured on **Athens Ga. Inside/Out**
IRS IRS6185 (US)   1987

OTHER COMPILATIONS

Gardening At Night
Featured on **Jamming! A New Optimism**
Situation 2 SITU11 (UK)   December 1984

Ages Of You
Featured on **Live! For Life**
IRS IRS5731 (US)   July 1986
IRS MIRF1013 (UK)   July 1986

Deck The Halls
Featured on **Winter Wonderland** (promo only)
Warner Bros Pro-A-3328 (US)   December 1988

It's The End Of The World As We Know It (And I Feel Fine)
Featured on **Greenpeace – Rainbow Warriors**
Geffen GHS2346 (US)   June 1989
BMG PL74065(2) (UK)   June 1989

COLLABORATIONS

Hindu Love Gods
Gonna Have A Good Time Tonight/Narrator
IRS IRS52867 (7") (US)   1986
(Bill Berry, Peter Buck & Mike Mills, with Warren Zevon on piano and Bryan Cook singing)

Full Time Men
I Got Wheels/One More Time*/Way Down South
Fast Is My Name (12" EP)
Coyote TTC8562 (US)   1986
(Keith Strong of The Fleshtones with Peter Buck on guitar; *Mike Mills plays organ)
I Got Wheels/High on Drugs
Featured on **Your Face, My Fist**
Coyote TTC88138 (US)   1988
(Peter Buck plays guitar)

Jason And The Scorchers
Both Sides Of The Line*/Hot Nights In Georgia†
Featured on **Fervor** (12" EP)
EMI America EE24 00801 (UK)   1984
(*Michael Stipe co-wrote; †Michael Stipe sings backing vocals)

Golden Palaminos
Omaha
Celluloid SCEL56 (7")/CEL183 (12") (US)   1985
(Michael Stipe sings lead vocals)
Boy (Go)
Celluloid SCEL58 (7") (US)   1985
(Michael Stipe co-wrote and sings lead vocals)
Boy (Go)/Clustering Train/Omaha
Featured on **Visions Of Excess LP**
Celluloid CELL6118 (US)   1985
(Michael Stipe sings lead vocals on all three songs and co-wrote Clustering Train and Boy (Go))

Warren Zevon
Sentimental Hygene LP
Virgin 90603 (US)   June 1987
Virgin V2433 (UK)   June 1987
(Bill Berry, Peter Buck & Mike Mills provide instrumentation on eight of the ten songs, co-wrote Even A Dog Can Shake Hands; Michael Stipe sings backing vocals on Bad Karma)

10,000 Maniacs
A Campfire Song
Featured on **In My Tribe LP**
Elektra 960738 (US)   August 1987
Elektra EKT41 (UK)   August 1987
(Michael Stipe sings duet with Natalie Merchant)

Natalie Merchant, Michael Stipe, Mark Bingham and The Roches
Little April Shower
Featured on **Stay Awake LP**
A&M SP3918 (US & UK)   1988
(One-off performance on Various Artists Walt Disney tribute LP)

Indigo Girls
Kid Fears*/Tried To Be True†
Featured on **Indigo Girls LP**
Epic 45044 (US)   March 1989
CBS 4634911 (UK)   March 1989
(*Michael Stipe sings backing vocals; †Bill Berry, Peter Buck & Mike Mills provide instrumentation)

Syd Straw
Future 40's (String Of Pearls)
Featured on **Surprise LP**
Virgin 91266 (US)   June 1989
(Michael Stipe sings duet and co-wrote)

PETER BUCK has supplied guitar on records by the following artists:

The Replacements
I Will Dare from **Let It Be LP** (Twin Tone TTR 8441 (US); Zippo ZONG 002 (UK) 1984. Also Twin Tone TTR 8440 (12") (US))

The Dream Academy
The Party from **Dream Academy LP** (Warner Bros 25265 (US); Blanco Y Negro BYN6 (UK) 1985)

The Fleshtones
Wind Out (REM composition) from **Speed Connection II LP** (IRS ILP26412 (UK) 1985)

Robyn Hitchcock
Chinese Bones and **Flesh Number One** from **Globe Of Frogs LP** (A&M SP5182 (US); A&M AMA5182 (UK) 1988)
Queen Elvis LP A&M SP5241 (US)

Drivin' 'n' Cryin'
Mystery Road LP (Island 91226 (US) 1989)

Nigel And The Crosses
Wild Mountain Time from **Time Between LP** (Byrds Tribute Album)
(Imaginary Illusion 004)

BILL BERRY
Into The Night from **New Experience LP**
(Illuminous June Records   1988)
(Bill Berry plays drums)

My Bible Is The Latest TV Guide/Things I'd Like To Say
(Dog-Gone 13111 (US 12" only))
(Bill Berry solo single) under pseudonym 13111

BOOTLEGS

As discussed elsewhere many R.E.M. bootleg LPs are of poor quality and of unspectacular performances. The following, however, all contain interesting material from a historical point of view:

Chronic Murmurings (double): Contains 1980 'Tyrone's' demos and 1982 RCA demos, amongst other items.

So Much Younger Then: 1981 Tyrone's show; all songs subsequently unreleased. (A number of songs from this show are on other bootlegs; this is the best collection)

Smokin' In The Boys' Room: Among live cuts, contains Mitch Easter's 'Radio Dub' mix of Radio Free Europe.

VIDEOS

R.E.M. Succumbs
Compilation of promo videos 1983–1986, and '**Left Of Reckoning**'. A&M video.

Athens, Ga – Inside/Out
Documentary on Athens. Includes R.E.M. Music and interviews.

■ (Peter Anderson)

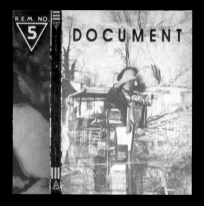